TOO BUSY
TO LIVE

THE ADDICTION AMERICA APPLAUDS

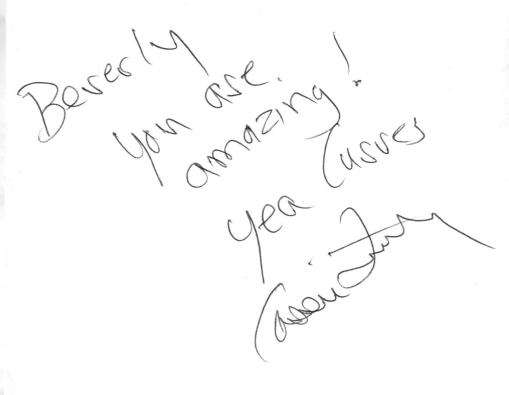

TOO BUSY TO LIVE

THE ADDICTION AMERICA APPLAUDS

Dr. Rick Fowler
and
Cassie Findley

with
J. Ray Smith

Fair Havens Publications®

Gainesville, Texas

Unless otherwise indicated, Scripture quotations used in this book are from the *Holy Bible*, New International Version (NIV). Copyright ©1973, 1978, 1984 International Bible Society. Used by permission of Zondervan Bible Publishers.

Scripture quotations marked (NLT) are taken from the *Holy Bible*, New Living Translation, copyright © 1996. Used by permission of Tyndale House Publishers, Inc., Wheaton, Illinois 60189. All rights reserved.

The B.A.L.A.N.C.E. acrostic outline in Chapter 2 was adapted from a sermon by Dr. Rick Warren, Pastor of Saddleback Church, Lake Forest, California, and used by permission. He is not responsible for the content of that section.

Material in this book is for the purpose of general information only. It is not the intention of the authors to give specific psychological or emotional counseling, medical, nutritional or physical fitness advice. It is their intention to provide information that will help the reader to understand some of the issues in these areas and to make better informed choices when pursuing options. For specific psychological or emotional problems, it is recommended that help be sought from a pastor or professional counselor, as the case may require. In the area of nutrition, a qualified nutritionist should be consulted to determine individual needs and conditions. Before beginning any program of physical fitness, one should consult a qualified health care provider for a thorough examination, and a qualified physician for diagnosis of specific complaints or questions about health.

Cover design and graphics by Cristina Fernandez-Mershon, Seattle, Washington
Manuscript design and format by Michelle VanGeest, Grand Rapids, Michigan
Sketches of Cassie Findley's cardio/strength training exercises by Donna Sullenger

ISBN 0-9664803-5-X

Library of Congress Control Number: 2004108719

Printed in the United States of America

Fair Havens Publications®
P. O. Box 1238
Gainesville, TX 76241-1238
Web Site: www.fairhavenspub.com

Rick Fowler

To my colleague, Harold Windus,
who became my first mentor over thirty years ago.
His consistent modeling of the balanced life principle
was the inspiration for this book.

Cassie Findley

To my husband, Bobby, who loves me unconditionally,
and my daughters, Clarisa and Shelbi, who remind me daily
about the meaning of true joy.

We are merely moving shadows,
and all our busy rushing ends in nothing.
We heap up wealth for someone else to spend.
And so, Lord, where do I put my hope?
My only hope is in you.
Psalm 39:6-7 (NLT)

Table of Contents

About the Authors

Dr. Rick Fowler

Dr. Rick Fowler is the Executive Director of Prestonwood Counseling Center in Dallas, Texas. He holds a doctoral degree in social psychology. Over the last 30 years, Dr. Fowler has served at several colleges as a professor of psychology, head basketball coach, and athletic director.

Various corporations and professional sports teams have contracted for his services as a consultant and management trainer. He is the author of over ten books, including *Together on a Tightrope, Honey, Are You Listening?*, and *Steps to a New Beginning*, winner of the Gold Medallion Award.

Additionally, Dr. Fowler has been featured at many seminars, workshops, and as a guest on "Focus on the Family" with Dr. James Dobson, "Insight for Living" with Dr. Charles Swindoll, and the "700 Club" with Pat Robertson.

Rick and his wife, Jeri, have been married for over thirty-six years and have two married children, Jodi and Chip.

Cassie Findley

Serving as the Director of Continuing Education and Research for Curves International, Cassie Findley is responsible for researching and teaching classes on kinesiology and nutrition. She has done extensive study in stress management and physical, emotional and spiritual wellness. She holds a Master of Science, Education Degree in Health Promotion. Dedicated to helping others understand the value of a balanced Christian lifestyle, Cassie held the positions of Assistant Dean for Student Life and Director of Health Education and Wellness during her fifteen-year tenure at Baylor University in Waco, Texas. With 26 years of experience in the health and fitness industry, she is certified by the Cooper Clinic in Dallas, Texas and Aerobic Fitness Association of America. Balancing active professional, civic, and family responsibilities, Cassie is a former school board member, a trainer for the Governor's Mentoring Initiative—Mentor Texas—and a presenter for the American College Health Association. The proud parents of Baylor University students, Carisa and Shelbi, Cassie and her husband, Bobby, are active members of Highland Baptist Church in Waco.

J. RAY SMITH

As President of Fair Havens Publications, J. Ray Smith is no stranger to a demanding schedule. His experience as a pastor and Bible college department chairman gives him biblical, spiritual insights into the issues of life management. He is a graduate of Samford University, Birmingham, Alabama (BA), New Orleans Baptist Theological Seminary (ThM) and Dallas Theological Seminary (STM).

Foreword

Too Busy to Live is a title for our times. It is common these days to see and hear advice to the busy in books, on radio and television, even in multitudes of email messages—all of which, of course, only contribute to our "busy-ness!"

The authors have written a well thought out and researched book of counsel and practical application for people caught up in the hectic pace of today's society. Beginning with an interesting correlation of human history to church history, they help to explain why and how Christians have been swept along with the masses. Their treatise on stress is explanatory and comprehensive. The information they share on adopting appropriate eating and exercise habits is helpful and reasonably adaptable.

For those of us interested in committing ourselves to a balanced lifestyle that will promote health and energy, productivity and longevity, *Too Busy to Live* is a timely roadmap to exactly that. For Christians who perceive their lives [to be] out of control as a result of the myriad demands...constantly being made on them and desiring a peaceful lifestyle that will enable them to serve, honor and glorify Christ, many of the answers are available within these pages.

Zig Ziglar
Author and Motivational Teacher

Introduction

An addiction is sweeping our country; but little is being done to stop it. There is no government task force to study the problem, no commission headed by a "Czar" to combat it. There are few expressions of concern from our pulpits. In fact, most businesses and major corporations encourage or require their employees to indulge themselves freely in this addiction. Even most church leaders commend their members who have fallen into it and exhort others to follow their example.

This addiction is not to a drug or any substance. It is not to anti-social or what is considered immoral behavior. Yet, it can be just as destructive. It is a behavioral disorder that presents itself as compulsive, excessive busy-ness.

Excessive busy-ness fits the current definition of an addiction. In the past, the definition of an addiction was limited to continued excessive use of drugs or other substances such as alcohol or tobacco. Recently, the definition has expanded to include compulsive destructive behavior, such as gambling, promiscuous sex or viewing pornography. The term, addiction, derives from the Latin word that means "given over." A good definition of addiction is "giving oneself habitually and compulsively to substance abuse or destructive behavior in spite of negative consequences."

Busy-ness is excessive when it throws one's life out of balance. Excessive busy-ness crowds one's life with activities and clutters it with too many minute details to the point of distracting attention from what should be the focal point of meaningful, purposeful living. To be busy being industrious, productive and diligent in managing responsibilities is, of course, a virtue; but if one is too busy to keep important priorities in proper perspective and is no longer able to control or manage how he spends most of his time, then he is too busy. When excessive busy-ness causes negative consequences and one continues the same behavior patterns, the busy-ness has become compulsive and destructive.

Society generally discourages addictions. For example, employers are reluctant to hire someone with a history of drug abuse or alcoholism unless the individual can give assurance that he has recovered from the addiction. A church member addicted to sexual promiscuity is likely to be confronted by church leaders and possibly subjected to church discipline.

Busy-ness addiction is a notable exception to society's rules. 21st century Western culture defines success, status, loyalty and purpose in terms of a high volume of activity. The unhealthy negative consequences of excessive busy-ness go largely unrecognized or are attributed to other causes. Instead of identifying busy-ness addicts as workaholics, the culture calls them "winners." Unrestrained and undisciplined desires are no longer regarded as sins. That idea has been replaced by the adage, "You can have it all." Deferred gratification used to be considered a virtue and a way to "get ahead." The cultural consensus today is, "You can't know what the future will be, so live in the *now*." As a result, people try to fill each day with more activities than they can manage properly. Philosophically, the culture says, "Since there is no absolute truth, life can have no ultimate meaning or purpose." As a result, people are cramming their lives with activities, trying to find some experience that will give them a feeling of fulfillment and purpose, or, at least, distract them from thinking about the absurdity of their lives.

The consequences of busy-ness addiction can be disastrous. Physically, it can lead to chronic fatigue, heart attack, and susceptibility to infectious diseases. Emotionally, it promotes tension and stress, irritability and anxiety, often resulting in strained or broken relationships in the family. Psychologically, it can manifest as depression, narcissism, and perfectionist, compulsive behavioral disorders.

Introduction

In this book, the authors will explain why and how Western culture drives us to be excessively busy. Then they will contrast commonly held cultural ideas with timeless biblical principles for living a meaningful, purposeful life. Finally, they will describe the steps to recovery from busy-ness addiction and suggest practical changes in your lifestyle that will help to restore health and balance.

CHAPTER 1

Why Are We So Busy?

Harried Harry's day began at five o'clock. It was Friday, the day he hoped to sign the contract on his company's deal with the Grewing Corporation. He needed to get to the office early to make sure the papers were in order. Bagging the Grewing account would not only mean a nifty commission check, but also would enhance his image in the company as a "winner." It would be one more step toward the promotion he had been aiming for, or maybe even a chance to leverage himself into a better paying job with another company.

At the office his frustration flared into anger when his secretary did not finish on time a task he had given her. She tried to offer him an excuse: something about three executives bringing urgent, time-consuming work to the secretarial pool at the same time. But Harry thought, "She knew I needed those copies. I can't believe she just expected me to understand when she didn't have them ready for me."

The meeting with the Grewing people went reasonably well, but there were a few last-minute sticking points that would have to be resolved before the deal could be completed. A couple of paragraphs needed to be re-written, and then the whole contract would have to be checked to see if the changes affected other paragraphs that were cross-referenced. His boss had warned him not to send that kind of "grunt work" to the lawyer, so Harry decided to take the contract home on a disk and do the work himself over the weekend on his laptop. Then the lawyer could review it on Monday.

As Harry packed his briefcase to leave, his wife, Ellen, called from her office. "Mrs. Bloomfeld brought me a couple of folders of paperwork that has to be finished before I leave today. It's going to take another hour or so. Would you be a 'dear' and pick up the kids from day-care?"

"Sure, hon."

"Remember, we are going to that dinner party at the Johnsons tonight at 7:30, so pick up some food for the children on the way home."

Harry had been through this before, so he knew the drill. The timing would be close, but with careful planning he knew he could pull it off. He was leaving the office at 5:00, and the commute would take about 45 minutes. Making a couple of calls from the car on his cell phone, Harry ordered a pizza delivery to his home and arranged for the baby sitter to come early to supervise the kids' supper. That would give him time for a quick workout at the fitness center after dropping off the children at home. He was one short of his usual four workouts that week.

Feeling rather smug, Harry piled Ellen into the car just in time to make the 20-minute drive to the Johnsons' house. They would be "fashionably late," but that didn't bother Harry. It would give their friends the impression that they were busy and important people.

The dinner party went well for Harry and Ellen. Harry was bored at first when some of the older guests talked about the similarities between the 1987 stock market crash and the way the market seems to be headed today. "Things are different now from what they were back then. Besides, no one knows what the future holds, so why stew about it?" he thought. Finally he managed to steer the conversation to his job, mentioning his work on the Grewing deal and what it would do for his career when he closed on it the next week. Everyone congratulated him, some with barely concealed envy. "It doesn't get any better than this," he told himself.

Likewise, Ellen found an opportunity to comment on the excel-

lent working conditions at her new job. "When I stayed late today to finish some important paperwork, the Vice President said she is recommending me to be the office manager. The last person to hold that job was promoted to 'Account Executive' with a nice raise in salary plus a commission." Her friends were duly impressed.

On the way home, Harry and Ellen made plans for how they would spend their increased incomes. Even though they were both earning substantial paychecks, there never seemed to be quite enough money. Harry was amazed recently when he figured out how much they were paying in taxes. Ellen's job pushed them into the 30% tax bracket. But a newsletter article he had read proved that the average American family pays at least 50% of their income in taxes when all the other taxes are added to the income tax, such as property tax, sales tax, and gasoline tax. He was amazed when he examined his telephone bill carefully, something he had not done until lately. It was loaded with taxes.

"Ellen, I hate to say it, but it takes most of one of our incomes just to pay our taxes. And then there is day care. It's a good thing we are getting raises. Now maybe we can afford to take that dream vacation we have been talking about, and buy that plasma big-screen high definition television we saw at the mall. Our old set is obsolete!"

"Yes, and I would like for us to consider a larger house. Where would I put that TV in our little den? There is barely room for the entertainment center we have now."

"Right! Maybe we could have a room just for a home theater."

"Do you really think we can afford all that now, Harry?"

"I don't see why not. The Grewing deal will increase my salary enough for the larger house payments. We can charge the TV on our credit card and pay it off when you get your raise."

"Oh, Harry, this is so exciting! I can hardly wait to tell our friends what we are doing."

Saturday was another full day. Harry got up early and ate breakfast at a local restaurant with the men's fellowship group from his church. Then he hurried home to mow the lawn before leaving with some friends for the ballpark. There was a big game that afternoon. It would be a long night, because he had to finish the Grewing contract before Sunday.

Sunday morning came too soon for Harry. He had been up late, working. Ellen understood how important the Grewing deal was, so she hadn't tried to talk to him when he returned from the game. He had mentioned something about being seen on television and then shut himself up in his office until after midnight.

They usually attended the early service at church to give them time for a round of golf after their Sunday brunch. Harry had been working on his swing, and was eager to try out the new techniques he had learned. They were playing against their friends Bill and Janet. The last time they played, Bill finished ahead of Harry with two under par. "Not today!" Harry promised himself as he remembered the last game. Bill was not a very good winner, and Harry was a lousy loser. This would be a fight to the finish.

Harry was in a great mood, even though he was "feeling a little tired" when he and Ellen returned to the church for the evening service. His new swing technique had paid off. The birdies had flown around him, but Bill was haunted by the bogeys. He just had to stay a while after the service to "fellowship" with his buddies and celebrate his victory.

When they finally arrived at home, the children needed their baths to get them ready for school on Monday. The bedtime rituals took about forty minutes after that. Harry and Ellen collapsed exhausted into their bed at about eleven. Harry murmured to Ellen, "What a great week-end! I'll set the clock for 5:00. We have another big week ahead of us."

• • • •

Harry and Ellen are an imaginary couple, but you probably found some things in common with them. Although they are Christians who attend church faithfully, the way they think, make decisions and act is determined more by Western culture than by biblical principles. What is it about our culture that seems to make people so busy, driven, insecure, angry, competitive, shallow, pleasure seeking, and "now" oriented?

The reasons for our busy-ness are the results of a complex series of interrelated developments extending 2,000 years into the history of Western culture. First we will examine the events and trends separately, and then finally show how they all connect to produce our American culture in the 21st century. If you are in a hurry to get to the practical applications of this book, you might want to skip to Chapter 2; but if you will take the time to read this chapter now, it will give you a perspective on our culture that will clarify the issue of busy-ness addiction. Occasionally, references will be made to this chapter in the rest of the book.

THE FULLNESS OF TIME

"But when the fullness of the time was come, God sent forth his son..." the apostle, Paul, wrote in Galatians 4:4. Roman civilization in the beginning of what we now call the first Christian century was at a turning point in its history. The might of Roman armies had established the *pax romana,* a time of peace and stability rarely seen in the ancient world. Technological developments in construction, such as the invention of concrete, made possible the erection of magnificent buildings in large metropolitan areas, connected by a network of roads, some of which are still in use to this day. The spread of the Greek language made communication free and open on a scale unmatched since the tower of Babel.

But all was not well. The moral underpinnings of Roman society were in decline. Gone were the ancient doctrines of responsibility and loyalty to family and tribe. The traditional pantheon of Roman gods, though still honored publicly in speeches by politicians, was not taken seriously by the average sophisticated Roman citizen. The uncertainties of Greek philosophy had taken its place. Into this spiritual vacuum moved the Eastern mystery religions and Gnosticism. These three belief systems had a common thread. They all taught some form of dualism, which considered matter to be evil and the soul or spirit to be good. The Orphic mysteries, for example, taught that matter corrupts the soul, and salvation is the soul's release from the body and material incarnations.

Julius Caesar's successor, Augustus, tried to rekindle belief in the old tribal gods as a basis for Roman unity, but to no avail.

Some of his devotees instituted an emperor worship cult, but Romans never regarded it as anything more than an affirmation of loyalty to the government. His final solution was to organize a giant governmental bureaucracy that provided social welfare and public spectacles to entertain the restless masses. Although his system lasted for well over two hundred years, it only slowed the inevitable dissolution of the empire.

REASONS CHRISTIANS WERE PERSECUTED

Christians' refusal to worship any other gods than the God of the Jewish and Christian scriptures appeared to Roman officials as treasonous and an impediment to their attempts to unify the empire. In A.D. 64 the emperor, Nero, began to persecute Christians in Rome. The apostle, Paul, was one of his victims. His actions set a precedent that continued sporadically in various local areas until the year 250 A.D. The emperor, Decius, in 249 A.D. issued an imperial edict requiring all citizens of the empire to sacrifice to the old Roman gods. For the first time Christians were persecuted for their faith throughout the empire. The reason Rome persecuted Christians and not the followers of numerous cults and religions of the day was because their faith in divine revelation through Christ and the apostles gave them a standard of absolute truth by which even the state could be measured. Rome at that time would not accept an authority higher than the state. The persecutions continued off and on until 313 A.D. when the emperor, Constantine, instituted an edict of toleration for the Christian faith after his own conversion.

CHALLENGES TO CHRISTIANITY

Three of Constantine's sons who succeeded him favored Christianity far more than their father had. Even so, there was stiff competition for the souls of men and women from paganism, the Eastern cults, and from the cults of the barbarians who were infiltrating the empire.

A new religion called Neo-Platonism not only opposed Christianity but also influenced it. It would play a major role in shaping the culture of busy-ness. Combining the philosophy of Plato and Pythagoras with magic, numerology, Babylonian astrology and mysticism, it asserted that ultimate reality is in the immaterial realm of perfect forms or ideas. The phenomena, or particulars of the material universe (anything experienced by the senses), are impermanent, constantly changing. The universe was considered to be one vast organism, governed by reason or natural law, an idea taught by the Stoics. Augustine, Bishop of Hippo, was a student of Neo-Platonism before his conversion to Christianity. He never fully abandoned its teachings and was instrumental in introducing them into the church.

The greatest challenge to Christianity came from a secret society that worshiped a mysterious deity called Mithras, loosely associated with the Persian sun god, Mithra. Limited in membership to men, it appealed strongly to Roman soldiers who spread it throughout the empire.

Based on Plato's misconception that the earth is the center of the universe, Mithraism employed the principles of astrology to work out a plan of salvation for its devotees. Assuming that the sun revolves around the earth on a path called the "celestial equator" (because it is equidistant from the equator on the earth's surface), it would intersect the Zodiac at two points. The Zodiac is a string of constellations in the night sky that, when viewed from the perspective of the earth, appear to form a belt or circle around the earth.

The ancients carefully noted where the celestial equator intersected the Zodiac at the spring and winter solstices (the time when the hours of daylight begin to lengthen or shorten). In 128 B.C. the Greek astronomer, Hipparchus, observed that, over time, the position changed. (Astronomers now know that this change is due to a "wobble" in the earth's rotation on its axis.) Given their belief in an immovable earth at the center of the universe, the only explanation for the sun's changing position at the solstices was that a "force" powerful enough to move the entire universe was shifting it.

This shifting of the sun's position at the spring solstice is apparently the source of the name for the modern "New Age" movement. In the Graeco-Roman period the sun had moved from the sign of Taurus, the bull, to Aries, the ram. David Ulansey in *The Origins of the Mithraic Mysteries* (Oxford University Press) suggests that was probably the reason Mithraic temple art depicted Mithras as slaying a bull. He was ending the old age of Taurus and bringing in the new age of Aries. In the 21st century, the sun's position at the spring solstice is gradually moving out of the sign Pices, the fish, and is approaching the "New Age of Aquarius" (the water bearer, often symbolized by a cup).

Hipparchus' discovery had profound implications for people steeped in dualistic and astrological belief systems. Dualism teaches that spirit or mind is pure and good; matter is contaminated and evil. Whatever is farthest away from the earth (or matter) is the purest spirit. Therefore, the stars, which are the farthest visible objects from the earth, were associated with deities and thought to be in the realm of pure spirit. The Neo-Platonists theorized that there is a realm of ideas, forms and pure reason that transcends the material universe. The earth was the passive receptacle on which the perfect forms make their impressions. That combination of beliefs reinforced the astrologer's conviction that the position of the stars and the planets at the time of a person's birth determines the course of his life.

Therefore, if a god commanded a force powerful enough to move the universe, then surely he would be able to influence the stars and lesser deities for the benefit of his worshippers and to guide their souls safely through the celestial spheres to the heavenly realms after their deaths. Mithraism became the most widespread mystery religion in the Roman Empire, and probably would have become the dominant religion had Christianity not arisen to take its place. Ironically, some of the beliefs of Mithraism have persisted through history and their revival in the New Age movement challenges Christianity again in the 21st century. It is an important factor leading to the busy-ness of American culture.

Another formidable rival to Christianity was Manichaeism. Mani, its 3rd-century founder, intended to create a universal religion by combining elements from most of the religions of his day, including Iranian Zoroastrianism, Indian Hinduism, Babylonian cultic beliefs, Judaism, Christianity, Buddhism, and Taoism. Its unifying principle was Gnosticism.

Dualistic in nature, Gnosticism taught that matter is evil and the spirit is good. The creation of evil matter occurred only after the First Principle, pure spirit god, created a series of emanations called aeons or sons, each inferior to the one before it. (The apostle, Paul, wrote his letter to the Colossians to combat the Gnostic heresy that Jesus was just one of many aeons.) Eventually, one of these aeons, called the demiurge, became far enough removed from pure spirit that it could create evil matter.

Perhaps by a cosmic accident, a wave of the pure spirit washed out of the heavenly realms and landed in the dark, evil world of matter, remaining imprisoned there. That is a Gnostic concept of man's original sin. A savior was sent from the heavenly realm to rescue the fallen ones by imparting to them the knowledge that they are part of the divine spirit. Included in the revelation of knowledge were rituals and initiations that would put the seekers into contact with the aeons or spirit guides, who could impart the knowledge needed to find their way back to the heavenly realm of the spirit from whence they came.

Missionaries of Manichaeism spread the aspiring universal religion throughout the ancient world, even to China in the East. From Egypt it swept across North Africa and reached Rome in the early 4th century. The church father, Augustine, accepted the teaching for a time until he converted to Christianity. It peaked in the 4th century in the Roman Empire, penetrating southern Gaul and Spain. As Christianity grew in popularity and power, Manichaeism began to wane. By the 6th century, it had died out as an organized religion in the Empire except for a brief revival in the Middle Ages. Nevertheless, its teachings survived, and continue to be disseminated by the theosophists and New Age proponents in the 21st century.

THE CHURCH VICTORIOUS?

In spite of its many rivals, Christianity became the Empire's state religion by 381 A. D., and the faith of the overwhelming majority of people in the Roman Empire by the end of the 5th century. Ostensibly, the triumph of Christianity over paganism was an opportunity to reshape the declining Roman culture into a society infused with the pure teachings of Christ and the apostles. Unfortunately, many of the converts were so steeped in Greek philosophy, teachings of the mystery religions and the concept of dualism, that they brought these pagan ideas into the church. The 1st century Christian faith became distorted. The authority of the church took precedence over the scriptures.

That compromises were made is evident by the way Christians named and timed their most sacred holy days. The celebration of Christ's resurrection was called Easter, an adaptation of Ishtar, the Babylonian fertility goddess associated with Tammuz, who died and rose again in sympathy with the seasonal death and revival of vegetation.

When setting a date to celebrate the birth of Christ each year, the church had to make a decision. There is no certainty as to the year of Christ's birth, not to mention the month and day. The church fathers chose a date that had been revered as a holy day by pagans for centuries. It was the date they celebrated the supposed annual resurrection of Tammuz. Later, it was the time in Roman society for the Saturnalia celebration and the traditional birthdays of Mithras and the sun cult god, Sol Invictus. It was the winter solstice, December 25 (in the pre-Julian calendar).

THE CHURCH DIVIDED

A serious distortion of biblical Christianity occurred when the church began to distinguish between sacred and secular, clergy and laity. This idea was based on the dualism of Neo-Platonism and Gnostic asceticism. Assuming that matter is evil, those who labor with and for material goods were regarded as inferior to those who took vows of poverty and devoted most of their time to prayer, meditation and the study of spiritual truths.

The first to write about this view was Eusebius, bishop of Caesarea and church historian in the latter third and early fourth centuries. He taught that there are "two ways of life" in the church. The "perfect life" is devoted to spirituality and contemplation and is practiced by priests, monks and nuns. The "permitted life" is secular and characterized by action such as serving in the army, administering government, farming, trading, and rearing children. This elitist view limited the concept of Christian calling to a small minority of believers. We will see later how the loss of a biblical concept of calling contributes to today's frantic busy-ness.

Monasticism was a logical expression of this two-tier approach to life and work. At first, individuals living in Egypt and the Middle East decided to withdraw from society and live a contemplative life as hermits. Beginning in the 3rd century in Egypt, the Christian monastic movement began. Although many individuals joined the movement out of a sincere desire to avoid the corruption and compromise that had crept into Christendom, its impetus was not based on the Bible. In Babylon and Persia the monastic movement patterned after the Manichean monasteries, following the asceticism of Buddhist and Hindu monks. An example of extreme asceticism was Simeon Stylites, who lived for thirty-six years on top of a pillar near Antioch—flies and other vermin swarming about his body.

THE CHURCH AND POLITICAL POWER

From approximately 500 until about 1400 A.D. the Christian church filled the power vacuum left by the decline and fall of the Roman Empire. Although the lofty ideals and high standards that Jesus and the apostles taught were not attained in society as a whole, several positive developments did occur during the so-called Middle Ages.

The church saved much of the Empire from anarchy by perpetuating Roman law tempered with Christian ideals. In the area of economics the church sought to limit and control greed and exploitation. Usury laws limited interest rates. Other laws forbade price gouging and withholding of goods from the market during times of scarcity. Although some of them were not consistent with a free market economy, they were honest attempts to base economic theory on the principle of love for one's neighbor. The church honored honest labor and skilled craftsmanship. Whether prestigious or menial, a man's job was considered his responsible service to the best interests of the community. For those who were too old or sick to work, the church built hospitals and other charitable organizations to care for their needs. Funding for these projects came from private citizens who considered giving to charity part of their social responsibility. Although it is impossible to turn back the clock, and no clear-thinking person would want to, we need to reclaim some of the principles that operated during this period of our history if we hope to escape the pattern of purposeless busy-ness that dominates 21st century culture.

In politics, the church promoted limitation of governmental authority and responsibility. By combining church and state, the worldly power of the state would be limited by and held accountable to ecclesiastical authority. That was a major improvement for the rights of the individual compared to the unchecked tyranny of the Roman Caesars.

THE CHURCH IN THE WORLD AND OF THE WORLD

Unfortunately, there were more compromises in the church's theology that would have disastrous effects. Until the 13th century Christian scholars had maintained a sharp distinction between philosophy and theology, even though theology had already been influenced by pagan categories and theories. Then the Scholastics abandoned the distinction altogether and attempted to create a Christian philosophy by taking the best of pagan philosophy and combining it with Christian theology.

The hinge for this turn of events was the re-discovery of Aristotle's writings through contact with the Arabians. Many scholars produced translations, the most notable being William of Moerbeke, who collaborated with Thomas

Aquinas. As Augustine introduced Plato's philosophy to the church through his lingering attachment to Neo-Platonism, Aquinas introduced Aristotle's philosophy into the academic circles of the church.

Aquinas' deviation began with his inadequate understanding of man's fall into sin. He theorized that only man's will is fallen, and not his intellect. Therefore, he thought, man can reason his way back to God. Aquinas felt free to use Greek philosophy as an aid in the process, assuming that his intellect or reason would enable him to choose what is helpful and eliminate the paganism that is not consistent with Christian thought.

A student of Plato, Aristotle accepted Plato's concept of the ideal forms, but he focused on their relationship to the particulars of the material world. (We would say data or information from observation.) By studying the way particulars react when the same set of circumstances is repeated, Aristotle taught, man can observe patterns that reveal the nature of the ideals or forms.

With that information, man can begin to understand how the universe works. Thus, he was the first ancient writer to describe clearly what we now call the scientific method. He also expressed in incipient form the concept of evolution.

The problem that Aquinas created by approving of Aristotle's teaching for the church was that he placed human reason on an equal footing with divine revelation and the Bible. Aristotle's philosophy suggested a way to understand the universe by starting only with man's reason and the material world. If one accepts that premise, there is no need for divine revelation. Inadvertently, Aquinas had opened the door of the church to what became Renaissance humanism.

THE BIRTH OF HUMANISM

The fallacy of starting with particulars as a basis for knowledge is the impossibility of arriving at absolutes in the areas of morals, values and law. "Whatever is, is right," is the logical conclusion under such a system. Most importantly, man-centered materialism cannot discover meaning for human existence. Here is an important clue as to why we are so busy today. The endless, fruitless effort to give meaning to life keeps us busy.

Humanism became the guiding principle of the Renaissance, a period that lasted from the fourteenth to the 17th century. It was a reaction against the church's distorted view of man. Abandoning the robust, well-rounded view of man presented by the Bible, the church saw man from a Neoplatonic perspective. His spiritual relationship to God and his otherworldly destiny were emphasized. His natural condition was belittled and treated as if it did not matter. Asceticism and withdrawal from human society were held up as the ideal of man's personal development.

Humanism was a revival of interest in man in his natural state. It was an appreciation of the human form in art, the valuing of literature for its skill in construction and the enjoyment it gives, interest in nature and the desire to understand it. It was taking satisfaction in human achievement and confidence in man's ability to master the world and shape his own future.

In one sense, humanism was a product of the Christian faith. It was Christianity's belief in an orderly universe governed by predictable laws that made scientific inquiry feasible. For example, Roger Bacon, a Franciscan, helped to lay the foundation for modern science with his writings on the scientific method of investigation. Albertus Magnus, a Medieval scholar, was a keen observer and skillful cataloguer of natural life. Many humanists were Christians, such as Petrarch, one of its outstanding early proponents. Others were only nominal Christians who remained in the church but abandoned most of its core beliefs. By and large, however, humanism became a secular movement that opposed Christianity.

Early on, the humanists struggled to find a universal principle or anything to give meaning and purpose to the universe and man's existence in it. Their repeated failures soon led to the pessimistic conclusion that there is no meaning or purpose for human life and no basis for morality. The failure of humanism would set the stage for the purposeless rounds of busy activity that characterize American culture. We will see how in a mo-

ment, but first we need to consider a more positive development.

THE REFORMATION

In addition to the Renaissance, there was another reaction
to the church's teachings. The Reformation was a movement
that sought to bring the church back to its roots: the teachings
of Christ and the apostles. A forerunner of the Reformation was
John Wycliffe (c.1320-1384), who regarded the Bible as a
higher authority than the church. He produced an English
translation that put the Bible into the hands of ordinary church
members across Europe. John Huss (c. 1369-1415), a professor
at the University of Prague, objected to the church's humanistic teaching that man can perform works that merit the merits
of Christ. Instead, he advocated a return to the biblical doctrine
of salvation by faith alone in Christ's death and resurrection. He
also extended Wycliffe's view that every believer has access to
God without the mediation of a priest. Church leaders guaran-
teed him safe conduct to the Council of Constance in 1415.
After he spoke, they declared him a heretic and burned him at
the stake. In spite of church opposition, the views of Wycliffe
and Huss took hold in northern Europe and became the views
of the Reformation movement.

Perhaps the most significant individual in the Reformation
was Martin Luther (1483-1546). The main tenet of his writings
was that salvation is by grace alone through faith alone, apart
from man's works, and that the authority of the Bible is higher
than church traditions or decisions of councils. In effect, Luther
opposed many of the distortions that had infiltrated the church's
teachings for centuries.

On April 18, 1521, copies of his works were piled on a table
when he was called before the provincial legislature at Worms,
and Charles V, Germany's Holy Roman Emperor, asked him
to recant. He refused, unless the church leaders could show him
in the Bible where he was mistaken in anything he had written. Luther set the precedent that Protestants would obey the
Bible instead of any human authority that contradicts it. The

reformers, such as Ulrich Zwingli and John Calvin in Switzerland, and Cranmer in England followed the trail that Luther had blazed. Although Luther's aim had been to reform the Catholic Church, the actual result of his teachings was to divide the Church in Europe.

The rise of nation states and strong monarchs had preceded the Protestant Reformation. The reformers gave them an alternative to submission to Rome. The first nation to break with Rome was England under Henry VIII. Other nations, such as Switzerland, followed suit. The expectation was that each nation state would adopt its own form of Protestantism based on local issues. However, Protestantism went in so many different directions with its reforms, that there often was no consensus in many nations as to which form of Protestantism to adopt as the state religion. The result in most European nations was a separation of church and state with a secular state and many denominations in the church.

THE ENLIGHTENMENT

Also contributing to the secularization of Europe was the movement called the Enlightenment. It was the logical extreme of Renaissance humanism. Philosophically, it was totally man-centered. Its adherents imagined that they could create a perfect, utopian society by perfecting man.

Politically, the Enlightenment was the driving intellectual force behind the French Revolution, which began in 1789, and later, the takeover of the Russian Revolution by Lenin and Trotsky in October of 1917. In both instances the leaders of the state deliberately set out to "dechristianize" the nation. By the end of World War I in 1918, the process had been largely successful in most of Europe.

Other developments contributed to the decline of Christianity and the rise of humanism in Europe. In science, a significant shift occurred. Scientists before the seventeenth and eighteenth centuries believed in an open system. They understood that the universe is not all there is. Rather, they believed God exists in heaven, and is over and above His creation. At will, He intervenes and makes things happen or prevents them from happening. He gives order and meaning to the universe, and holds man accountable for his actions in it.

Later scientists came to believe in a closed system. The universe is all there is. In their minds, there was no place or need for God. The laws of cause and effect were thought to govern everything, including human psychology and sociology. They considered human behavior to be a conditioned response to environmental factors. Man became merely a part of the great cosmic machine, being no more than a machine himself. Sadly, in such a system, there is no place for such concepts as love, morality, or even freedom for the individual.

The single person most responsible for popularizing this view was Charles Darwin (1809-1882). In his book, *The Origin of Species,* he theorized that all life came into being through a mechanism called evolution. Specifically, the processes that supposedly make this system work are "natural selection" and chance, or random mutations.

Thomas Huxley promoted the theory and extended it from biology to sociology and even ethics. He coined the catch phrase, "survival of the fittest." Eventually this line of reasoning provided the rationale for Nazi racism and genocide in Germany.

THE DEMISE OF REASON AND HOPE

Another shift occurred in the area of philosophy. Before the 18th century, most non-Christian philosophers agreed on three things. First, they believed that man is capable of discovering universal principles, beginning with himself alone and analyzing particulars (information gained from observation). Second, they accepted reason as a valid method of arriving at truth. Third, they were optimistic. They believed that man would eventually succeed in discovering universals that give unity and order to the universe.

Four influential thinkers shifted away from this optimistic hope. By the 18th century it was clear to most humanists that their search for universals had been like groping around in the dark in a circular room with no exits. They gave up the idea that they would ever find unifying principles for the universe. The first was Jean-Jacques Rousseau (1712-1778).

Starting from the premise that man is good by nature, he inferred that the restraints of civilization corrupt him and rob him of freedom. The autonomous freedom that Rousseau sought was freedom, not only from God, but also from restraint of any kind, including culture, authority, or even human reason. It was an absolute freedom that places the individual at the center of the universe. Here is another important clue as to why we are so busy. Absolute freedom can keep a person quite busy exploring every option available.

His followers carried his philosophy to extremes. Robespierre, "King of the Terror" during the French Revolution, used Rousseau's political writings as a rationale for wholesale executions of those who refused to accept the will of the majority. In Britain, David Hume (1711-1776) downplayed reason as a way to know truth, and emphasized instead human experience and feeling. He even questioned cause-and-effect as a valid concept. In Germany, Rousseau inspired the romanticism movement, which sought to find meaning in self-expression, especially of the emotions. A prophet of revolutionary individualism, the Marquis de Sade (1740-1814) foresaw that individual expression unrestrained by reason or religion would result in uninhibited cruelty. His name became the basis for the term "sadism."

The second influential thinker was Immanuel Kant (1724-1804). This German philosopher attempted to create a theory of knowledge based on a combination of observation and reason. Through observation, he said, man can gather information about the particulars, and through reason he can make the inferences and connections that lead him to the ideals or unifying principles. Unfortunately, after exhaustive attempts, he finally concluded that man can know nothing about the ideals of meaning and value, the noumena, as he called them. Philosophy sank further into despair of ever finding meaning through reason.

The third influential thinker was Georg Wilhelm Hegel (1770-1831), also a German. The background of his philosophy was the Neo-Platonism of F. W. J. von Schelling and the theosophy of Jakob Boehme. Neo-Platonism taught that there is an ultimate One, the god that is behind all experience. The One encompasses both thought and objective reality, and can be known through mystical experience.

Hegel referred to the One as *Geist*, that is, Spirit or Mind. Reality is the evolution of Spirit as it unfolds and grows in self-consciousness. The dynamic pattern of this development is called Dialectic. The basic concept of rationalism was antithesis: if one idea (thesis) is true, then its opposite (antithesis) must be false. Hegel suggested that in some way and at some point, both thesis and antithesis could both be true, because everything is constantly changing and evolving into something different from what it was previously. This point of transition he called a synthesis. That synthesis would in turn become a new thesis with its implied antithesis and develop into another synthesis in an infinite process. The final result of this form of idealism is that the traditional understanding of objective truth and moral standards becomes meaningless, and everything is relative.

The last of the four influential thinkers was Soren Kierkegaard (1813-1855). Rejecting Hegel's idealism because it could not be proved and had no relationship to the reality of human existence, he offered another approach that is called existentialism. Like the philosophers before him, he despaired of arriving at meaning or universal principles through reason. He was even skeptical about man's ability to know anything based on historical information. His solution was to abandon reason totally and make a "leap of faith." Kierkegaard's faith was not based on any historical evidence (such as the birth, death and resurrection of Christ), but was simply faith in faith. Since reason by itself leads to pessimism and despair, man can only find positive meaning or hope in life by making a decision to exert his will and believe what he wants to be true even though it is not consistent with reason. It was a commitment to the absurd.

By the latter 19th century the prideful expectations of Renaissance man had come to a sorry end in Europe. Beginning with the assumption that unaided human reason is capable of finding meaning, purpose, and a unifying principle for the universe, humanists eventually reduced man to a mere machine, subjected him to unprecedented cruelty and humiliation, disparaged reason itself and finally committed intellectual suicide. A wall of separation had been established in the minds of 19th century intellectuals between reason (the "lower story" of objective observable information) and non-reason (the "upper story" of values, meaning and hope).

THE DEMISE OF TRUTH

This dichotomy was taught not only in the universities of Europe, but also in Christian colleges and seminaries. Kierkegaard introduced existentialism into Christian theology, and Karl Barth (1886-1968) promoted it. This rationalistic approach to theology denied the historicity of most of the Bible, especially its accounts of supernatural occurrences. Whatever truth the Bible contains, it is mainly in the area of non-reason, the "upper story," according to this view. In this way, humanistic distortions of the first century faith found their way into Protestant churches, just as they did earlier in the Roman Catholic Church.

THE GREAT AWAKENING IN AMERICA

But something very different was happening in the New World of the Americas during that period. Reformation Christianity took hold and flourished. At first, Christians were only a small minority of the colonists. But Protestant zeal for evangelism and outreach swelled their numbers. Beginning in the 1720s and lasting until after 1750, the revival movement called the Great Awakening spread through the thirteen colonies and established Christianity in general and Protestantism in particular as a prominent feature of American life and culture. The frontier revivals from the 1790s to the late 1830s and the work of volunteer societies such as the American Bible Society, the

American Sunday School Union and others seemed to fulfill the Protestants' dream of a Christian America. By the early 1830s, Alexis de Tocqueville of France observed during a visit to America, "there is no country in the world in which the Christian religion retains a greater influence over the souls of men."

In the area of economics, Puritans and others of the Reformed faith, especially Calvinists, practiced a kind of asceticism. It is sometimes referred to as the "Puritan work ethic." It taught that every Christian's job is a calling from God, and should be pursued conscientiously before Him. Whatever he produces should be for the good of the community. Idleness was considered a sin, as was spending one's earnings on selfish desires or luxuries. One should make as much money as he can, spend no more of it than is necessary, give to worthy causes, and save the rest. Under no circumstances should money be borrowed to fulfill personal desires. Later, we will see how the abandonment of Puritan economic principles has added to the pressure to be busy to excess.

Although some of these principles were based on an inadequate understanding of the Bible and were influenced by asceticism and legalism, they had a profound practical result. They were an effective formula for financial prosperity. Ironically, that financial success would eventually undermine the principles that helped to produce it.

WHEN AMERICA LOST ITS EVANGELICAL CHRISTIAN CONSENSUS

The evangelical consensus did not survive for long in America because a combination of developments tore it apart. Until the outbreak of the War Between the States in 1860, Christianity in America had been sheltered from the intellectual onslaughts that contributed to the decline of Christian culture in Europe. After the war, the writings of Charles Darwin and the rationalist and idealist philosophers found their way to American printing presses and the lecture halls of its universities. Protestant seminaries sent their professors to study in Europe, and they returned with a liberal form of Christianity that questioned its historical roots and the divine inspiration of the Bible.

Industrialization and urbanization brought new waves of European immigrants who came to America for economic, not religious, reasons. Most of them did not share traditional American evangelical beliefs. By the beginning of the 20th century, the dream of a Christian America was a fading memory. America was on the same path that led to the dechristianizing of Europe.

THE DEMISE OF THE PURITAN WORK ETHIC

The labor union movement eroded the Puritan work ethic. Because greedy capitalists exploited immigrants and other American workers through inadequate wages and inhuman working conditions, they organized themselves to negotiate for better treatment. No longer was labor considered a responsibility to contribute to the good of the community in the sight of God. Instead it became a commodity to be negotiated and sold to the highest bidder. Unionists sacrificed the interests of the larger community by withholding labor until their monetary interests were satisfied.

The industrial revolution further eroded what was left of the Puritan work ethic. Mass production of goods required mass markets of consumers. Capitalists realized that their best customers could be the workers who were producing the goods. Mass media such as newspapers, magazines, then radio, and eventually television informed the public of the new products that were becoming available. Not only did they inform, they also persuaded people that their lives were somehow incomplete without the products. Purchasing decisions were being made not on the basis of needs, but as a never-ending quest for fulfillment. Here is another clue to our busy-ness. We work longer and harder for more and more goods and services.

The standard of living in America continued to rise. After a depression in the 1930s, the economy came roaring back after World War II. With most of the factories in Europe in ruins, America was the only developed nation with its means of production intact. The generation of Americans that experienced the depression appreciated the value of a job and worked harder than ever to build financial security. With little competition, America became the wealthiest nation in the world.

In spite of the growing wealth, consumer spending could not keep up with production. Fractional reserve banking solved that problem by making easy credit available to consumers. Then it was no longer necessary to work and save for purchases. Americans became used to instant gratification of desires.

HIPPIES, HEROIN AND HINDUISM

Americans who lived through the Great Depression and World War II were content to enjoy the peace and prosperity of the post war economic boom and to rear their families. The latter they did exceptionally well, and produced the "baby boom" generation. "Boomers" were not content with the status quo. Many of them became either revolutionaries or dropouts from society. The "hippie" movement patterned after the bohemian idealist romanticists in Europe, giving vent to free expression of the individual. Many hippies used drugs, initially to find meaning in life through a mind-expanding experience of another dimension outside of conscious reason.

The drug culture was an outgrowth of the existentialism introduced by Kierkegaard and popularized by Karl Jaspers (1883-1969). Jaspers suggested that even though the rational mind sees life as absurd, it is possible to have a "final experience" that gives hope for meaning in life. To aid in finding this supra rational experience, an Englishman, Aldous Huxley (1894-1963), advocated the use of mind-altering drugs. The assumption was that there is no objective truth and everything is relative, so an individual can find his own truth inside his own head.

The drug culture naturally led to the next step in the escape from reason: Eastern mysticism. For millennia the Hindus have taught their followers that the meaning of life is not to be found in the world of the senses. The rational mind must be distracted by the chanting of mantras or transcendental meditation. When the sensate world has been blanked out in the mind, guided imagery leads the individual into experiences in a supra rational dimension.

Occult experiences follow the same pattern. Magic (or shamanism) assumes that power can be brought to bear on the rational, material world from an unseen supra rational realm through the performance of rituals and speaking certain words in the casting of spells. Through "mind over matter" one supposedly can create his own reality out of his own head.

Another name for the combination of pagan mysticism and the occult is the New Age Movement. For all practical purposes it is new packaging for the old Gnostic dualism and Hindu pantheism. Its main tenets are:

1. Man is god. Since he doesn't understand that he is god, he needs knowledge (*gnosis*) to raise his level of consciousness.

2. The earth is one vast interconnected organism (*Gaia*).

3. Spirit guides are available through channelers (mediums) to help man find his way to self-realization.

4. Life is a series of incarnations. If one lives a good life (good *karma*) he will be reincarnated at a higher level of existence, and the inverse is also true.

5. Ultimate salvation is for man's spirit to escape the spiral of incarnations in evil matter and to become one with the all-pervading spirit of the Brahma (*nirvana*). (Actually it means obliteration of the individual personality.)

Ironically, when Renaissance humanists abandoned traditional Christianity and sought to understand the universe through unaided human reason, it took them nearly 600 years to think themselves back to practically the same position held by many pagans in first century Rome. The dualism of Neo-Platonism and the Gnosticism of Manichaeism are firmly embedded in Western culture in the 21st century.

Postmodernism: A time of tolerance and political correctness

The term for the current period in Western thought is "postmodern." Renaissance and Enlightenment thinkers considered their time (from the fifteenth to the eighteenth centuries) to be the "modern period." Modernists rejected the Christian church and its traditions and sought to recapture the freedom and appreciation of man and his capabilities thought to characterize ancient Greek paganism before the Christian church triumphed over it in the Roman Empire. That is why they referred to the period dominated by Christianity as the Middle Ages (or even the "Dark Ages"). Their failure to discover a universally agreed upon objective basis for understanding reality and to usher in a perfect utopian society led to disillusionment. Postmodernism makes no pretense of appealing to reality or truth. It recognizes only two things: the autonomous self and the language he employs.

The self defines truth and reality. Utilizing the conscious, the unconscious and the subconscious, the whole person constructs his own understanding of truth and values. Since there is no objective standard for truth and everything is relative, the self is free to make any choice it likes. Reality outside of the autonomous self must be created with words. Assuming that there are no true propositions, the only question is the choice of words to create the desired impression or achieve the desired result. Words mean whatever the self wants them to mean. Instead of clear-cut definitions, there is a continuous interpretation of language in which each individual gets an equal vote.

When President Bill Clinton gave his deposition for the Monica Lewinsky hearings, he made what is now a famous statement, "…that depends on what the meaning of 'is' is…" Most Americans laughed it off as a clever attempt at legal maneuvering. However, it might have been a philosophical statement. It is perfectly consistent with postmodern thinking.

This instrumental view of language is the reason image is so important in American culture now. Language no longer communicates reality; it creates it. Image creates felt need and sales for products, forms social relationships, achieves promotion to positions in corporations, and elects politicians to office in government.

The result of postmodern thinking is "tolerance" and "political correctness." Like the government of the ancient Roman Empire, the one thing postmodernists cannot allow is the claim to have an absolute standard for truth. Each autonomous self must respect the other autonomous selves and allow them to have their own versions of reality. Everyone must have an equal voice.

A CULTURE SHAPED BY NARCISSISTS

Forget about ultimate concerns. The primary concern in American society is self-improvement. Frankly, that is probably the main reason you are reading this book. Roger Lundin suggests that most Americans are preoccupied with managing their experience and environment to achieve what he calls a "manipulatable sense of well-being." They focus on things that affect them personally that are under their control, such as understanding their own feelings, selecting healthy food to eat, physical fitness programs, time management, taking lessons to develop talents in music, dancing, or painting.

In fact, Americans have become so self-centered that what psychologists used to consider a neurosis has become a "normal" characteristic of the majority of people in this culture. It is called "narcissism."

The personality disorder gets its name from an ancient Greek myth. Narcissus was a handsome young man who caught the fancy of a nymph named Echo. When she approached to declare her love for him he rejected her cruelly. Other maidens suffered similar rebuffs. One of them prayed to the avenging goddess that Narcissus would someday feel what it is like to love but not have the affection returned. One day when Narcissus was hot and tired from hunting he came upon a beautiful clear fountain and a silvery pool of water sheltered by rocks, surrounded by lush grass. Stooping down to drink, Narcissus saw his reflection in the pool. He supposed it was a water spirit and became enamored. Every time he reached out to touch it, it vanished but soon returned to renew the fascination. He fell in love with the image of himself and could not turn away. Neither could he understand why the image would not return his love. Eventually he pined away and died by the pool. When the nymphs prepared a funeral pyre and came to retrieve his body, it could not be found. In its place was a flower with a purple center surrounded with yellow petals, which to this day preserves the memory of his name.

Most significant in Narcissus's story is that he failed to distinguish between something in his environment and himself. Psychologists refer to people who have similar difficulties as "narcissists." Sigmund Freud proposed the theory that all humans pass through a stage of narcissism in their development. In the mother's womb all of the baby's needs are met instantly. The temperature is always comfortable. Food is piped in continuously through the umbilical cord, so there is never a hunger pang. Waste is disposed of in a manner so efficient that it is not even noticed. His environment in his mother's body seems to be a part of him.

After birth, there is a dramatic change. The baby's needs are still met by the mother, but not always instantly. The baby still thinks of his mother as an extension of himself. Every time there is a delay in feeding or changing a diaper or finding a warm blanket, he becomes frustrated and angry. This delayed gratification creates ambiguous feelings in the infant toward the mother, because she is not only the nurturing provider that meets his needs, but also the one who frustrates him by withholding from him for a time whatever he needs or wants. The baby normally attains self-awareness at about eight months to one year and moves to the next stage of development.

Adults can regress and behave in an infantile manner, failing to distinguish other people from themselves. They see others as existing to meet their needs, and become angry when those needs are not met.

Christopher Lasch examines the mental and emotional state of what may be a typical American in his book, *The Culture of Narcissism: American Life in an Age of Diminishing Expectations.*

Here is a summarized partial list of characteristics he has observed:

1. *A sense of impending doom.* Americans expect something bad to happen eventually, such as nuclear war or ecological disasters like global warming and depletion of the ozone layer. Few people seriously think anything can be done to avert them.

2. *Interest in personal survival strategies.* People are looking for anything that will help them to live longer, be healthier and find peace of mind.

3. *Presentism.* Because Americans are losing their sense of historical continuity, they live for themselves in the present, not to honor their predecessors or to provide for their posterity.

4. *Dependency on institutions and other people.* Self-reliance has given way to the expectation that the state or the corporation will meet the individual's needs. Freedom from family responsibility makes him feel vulnerable. He relies on other people to be an admiring audience so that he can see himself reflected in their attention.

5. *Anger.* Outwardly docile and sociable, many Americans have a boiling rage inside with few legitimate outlets and little respect for authority figures.

6. *Emotional insecurity.* Americans are increasingly becoming anxious or depressed, with feelings of discontentment and emptiness. Secular therapists can offer little help because they have rejected traditional values that can offer any hope, such as love, duty and self-control.

7. *No limits to desires.* No matter how affluent Americans become, Madison Avenue advertising creates the desire for more and different things.

8. *Dread of old age and death.* Narcissists crave the admiration of others for qualities characteristic of youth: good looks, physical strength and boundless energy. It is a losing proposition. So also is the narcissist's view of death. The best he can hope for is absolute cessation of the constant stress and strain in his life in the oblivion of *nirvana.*

9. *Despair and resignation.* Preoccupation with personal growth is a substitute for faith.

10. *Winning images.* Success is no longer defined by performance or accomplishment. The appearance of success is what counts.

11. *Hedonism.* Pleasure is the motivation for most of what Americans do. Service to the community has little to do with one's job. Money itself is not the chief end. It is the pleasure that money buys.

12. *Stressful play.* It has been said that Americans worship their work, work at their play and play at their worship. They are forgetting how to play for fun. Competitiveness has degenerated into mutual exploitation, the attempt to get pleasure and satisfaction at someone else's expense. The concern for competent performance in play has become as serious and stressful as the workplace.

13. *Trivialization of sports.* While Americans take play too seriously, they do not take sports seriously enough. In the past sports created the illusion of reality by giving what would otherwise be insignificant activities serious meaning. By submitting to the rules of the game and decorum, players and spectators create a representation of life. The game is like the performance of a play. It is a fantasy. But players destroy the illusion when, perhaps to justify their large salaries, they publicly describe themselves as entertainers. Television turns spectators into participants by encouraging

them to mug for the camera, call attention to themselves with banners and bizarre behavior. In some instances, fans have intruded into the game by rushing onto the field of play or destroying parts of the stadium after a significant victory. When the rules are broken the spell is broken, and sports degenerate into mere spectacles, sometimes violent ones.

14. *Compulsion.* The narcissist's preoccupation with self and ceaseless self-scrutiny eventually threatens to overcome him with his own banality. He resorts to obsessive-compulsive behavior to avoid thinking about the absence of meaning and purpose in his life.

A NATION OF BUSY-NESS ADDICTS

This is the sad, declining culture modernism and its offspring, postmodernism, have produced. Let's review some of the high points of what we have learned so far and zero in on the factors in our culture that influence people to be so busy.

We are addicted to busy-ness because we do not have sufficient clear-cut goals and purpose for life itself. It has been said that a fanatic is one who doubles his effort after he has lost sight of his goal. If there is no objective reality and no universal meaning and purpose for human life, the postmodernist has no sure answer for the question, "Why am I here?" The job of creating his own reality and shaping his own purpose for life drives him to fanatical activity. By the way, the word "fanatic" literally means "inspired by a deity." Man has become his own god.

We are busy because time has become our enemy. Our culture places the most value on qualities possessed by the young. Every grain of sand that flows through the hourglass drains our most precious possessions. We spend many hours each week in exercise and fitness programs to slow the aging process. Death inexorably approaches with each passing moment. Without faith and hope for a better life beyond this one, death is the cut-off point, the end of everything we are desperately trying to keep for ourselves. Whatever we hope to get out of life must be done now.

We are busy because pleasure has become our primary motivation. But pleasure is like a drug. As soon as it wears off, you want more of it. The more you get of it, the more of it you need to get the same "kick."

We are busy because there is no limit to our desires. Mass media bombards us with information about new and better products. We have been trained and conditioned to consume. No matter how much we accumulate or use, there is always something else that we didn't know we needed. Instead of saving to meet future needs, we expect instant gratification. Out come the credit cards, and the interest calculators start running. We have to keep working longer and harder to earn the money to fulfill our insatiable desires.

We are busy because we have become dependent on institutions. Refusing to take family responsibility seriously, we have become vulnerable to the vicissitudes of life. Corporations will provide health insurance and government will create a "safety net" for us by taking care of disability and the costs of aging. The result is that half our income goes to taxes to fund the welfare entitlements and other costs, and more money that would have been part of our salaries goes to insurance companies.

Finally, we are busy because our lives are empty. Living mainly for one's self is a dreary business. Every idle moment must be filled with activity, even if it is just listening to music. We can't bear to have time to think about how desperately boring and meaningless our lives are.

Christian Busy-ness Addicts

But what about Christians in the church? Have we been affected by this culture? Perhaps we have, much more than we realize.

Imagine a place where everyone wears a lift in his left shoe: the "land of the limpers." A stranger arriving there for the first time thought it was odd for everyone to go limping through life. But, to fit in with society, he agreed to insert the lift into his own left shoe. At first it seemed awkward, but after some time passed, he got used to it and the limp no longer bothered him. Eventually, he forgot about the limp altogether. In the land of the limpers, limping was normal.

Most Christians are influenced by the culture the same way that everyone else is. We watch television, go to movies, read books, newspapers and magazines, see billboards, and talk with associates in the workplace. Gradually, almost imperceptibly, our way of looking at life changes. We pick up an idea from a sitcom on television, hear a suggestion on a radio talk show, see a subliminal message on a billboard while driving home from work. Eventually, the culture appears normal and right to us. We are doing essentially the same thing everyone else in the culture is doing. Our lives are just as full of stress and almost frantic busy-ness. We don't understand why we are living that way and don't know how to stop. Perhaps that is the way you feel now.

Before you continue reading, go back to page 19 and re-read the "Harried Harry" story in the light of this analysis of American culture.

CHAPTER 2

Off by Two Degrees

To FAIL TO PLAN IS TO PLAN TO FAIL.

So how can you prevent the cultural influences and stresses of life from forcing you into the frantic busy-ness pattern? First, you must develop a plan. Think of your life as a trip in an airplane. Before the plane ever leaves the ground, a pilot makes decisions about the cruising altitude, route, destination, fuel on board, and alternate airport. The flight plan keeps the plane on course regardless of reduced visibility, mountainous terrain, or adverse weather conditions.

To reach the intended destination, he sets a course heading for a certain degree. Flight instructors recommend that pilots locate a checkpoint in the first two minutes of a flight to make sure they are exactly on course. When making his first cross-country flight in a private plane, Dr. Fowler, distracted by nervousness, flew for thirty minutes before checking his course. A two-degree error quickly became a thirty-degree error when he failed to make the necessary correction for wind. When he reached what should have been his destination, he was over 20 miles away from where he was supposed to be, and could not locate the airport. Swallowing what was left of his pride, he had to turn around and fly back to where he started.

If you do not have a plan for your life and check it frequently to see if you are still on course, winds of life—the expectations of society and the "tyranny of the urgent"—will cause you to make what seem like small deviations. You do not plan to be trapped in a vortex of frantic busy-ness, but letting your life drift just two degrees off course can take you there.

HALF ASLEEP IN THE COCKPIT

One way our culture causes us to deviate from a wholesome life plan is sleep deprivation. God designed the human body to operate in cycles of sleep and wakefulness. Originally the pattern of daylight and darkness guided man's sleep habits. Although he had light from the hearth fire and oil lamps, its quality was poor and it was expensive to maintain. Most families did not stay up more than two or three hours past sundown. If they got up with the sun, they would get at least nine or maybe ten hours of sleep.

This ancient pattern changed dramatically when Thomas Edison invented the electric light bulb. Cheap, efficient and bright enough to make most activities enjoyable without eyestrain, this revolutionary light source made staying awake at night easy and attractive. Even so, most people continued to get at least eight hours of sleep each night, which is the amount most sleep experts recommend.

Other technological developments shortened sleep time. First radio, and then television offered entertainment to keep people up later at night. However, most stations in the early days of the broadcast industry signed off the air at about ten o'clock because the majority of the audience was going to bed then.

Today, people are awake all hours of the night. Shift workers are on the job at assembly lines that never stop. Truck drivers crisscross the interstate highway system throughout the night. Airlines offer travelers discounts to purchase tickets on "red eye" flights in the middle of the night. Stock traders in America are keeping up with the global markets in Europe and

Asia in "real time." Stores and restaurants stay open all night. Of course, the internet is available 24/7 for shopping, communicating and conducting business.

The end result is that Americans are sleeping less than ever. The National Sleep Foundation's annual "2001 Sleep in America Poll" suggests that 63% of American adults get less than eight hours of sleep per night. Thirty-one percent of the 1,004 adults over 18 years of age surveyed admitted sleeping less than seven hours on weeknights. Over one third of them said they are sleeping less now than they did five years ago. For most of them, the reason is long work hours. Thirty-eight percent of the respondents said they work 50 hours or more a week. Two thirds of those surveyed said they continue their normal activities even when they feel sleepy, disregarding the effects. That means that two out of every three Americans you encounter might not be fully awake.[1]

People imagine they accomplish more by spending less time sleeping. The fact is they are paying a high price for the time saved. There are many negative consequences of sleep deprivation. One is mental fatigue. Dr. Charles Pollak at Cornell University's New York Hospital in Westchester County warns that lack of sufficient sleep impairs the ability to think clearly and shortens the attention span. Other consequences are chronic tiredness, frequent irritability, poor job performance, and accidents in industry and on the highways. The U.S. Department of Transportation estimates that up to 200,000 traffic accidents every year could be the result of sleep deprivation.[2]

Perhaps your lack of sleep results from activities other than work. Do you stay up watching television when you could go to bed? Are you scheduling too many social activities during the week? Do you have a consistent routine to prepare your children for bed, and a time deadline for starting it every night?

A few simple changes in lifestyle also can help. Since exercise is stimulating and invigorating, plan to finish any activity involving strenuous exercise, such as working out, at least two to three hours before bedtime. Avoiding caffeine after four in the afternoon is helpful if you have difficulty falling asleep.

Finishing dinner at least two hours before bedtime and limiting the amount of food consumed facilitates going to sleep on time. If you feel hungry at bedtime, a glass of warm milk sweetened with a half teaspoon of honey will satisfy your hunger and help you relax. If you have difficulty digesting milk, try boiling it gently for ten seconds then drink it after it cools down. Milk is a natural source of nutrients that have a calming effect, such as calcium, magnesium and tryptophan. The slow-burning honey helps to keep your blood sugar level from dropping.

Some people resort to using alcohol at bedtime as a sedative to help them calm down and go to sleep. Although it can make you drowsy at first, its high caloric content acts like fuel in your body's system and literally "fires you up" after the initial effects wear off, causing you wake up later in the night. You will be better off if you give up the "night cap." The same principle applies to bedtime snacks that are high in refined sugar or simple carbohydrates, such as donuts, cake and most cookies.

Rather than trying to cheat your body out of the rest the Creator designed it to need, consider limiting or eliminating some of the activities that deprive you of sufficient sleep. The late Vince Lombardi once said, "I think good physical conditioning is essential…A man who is physically fit performs better at any job. Fatigue makes cowards of us all." The Bible condones industry, discipline and hard work, but it also cautions that even these good habits can be taken too far. Evaluate your work habits and goals to determine if they are consistent with biblical principles. "Unless the Lord builds the house, its builders labor in vain…In vain you rise early and stay up late, toiling for food to eat—for he grants sleep to those he loves."(Psalm 127:1-2) An alternate reading for the last phrase is "for while they sleep he provides for those he loves."

If your work prevents you from getting at least the minimum eight hours of sleep you need every night for good mental and physical health, then your life is out of balance. When you balance work with adequate rest, you will find it much easier to keep your life on course. Rick Warren, Pastor of Saddleback

Church in Lake Forest, California, has designed an acrostic arrangement of Bible verses that can help you achieve balance in your work. The comments and explanations are ours.

WHAT IS B.A.L.A.N.C.E.?

<u>B</u>uilding your life around Christ.

> *"So do not worry, saying, 'What shall we eat?' or 'What shall we drink?' or 'What shall we wear?' For the pagans run after all these things, and your heavenly Father knows that you need them. But seek first his kingdom and his righteousness, and all these things will be given to you as well..."*
> *(Matthew 6:31–33)*

Ask yourself, "Are the long hours I work the result of building my life around my job, profession or business instead of Christ?" What do you consider to be the source of your income and security: your work or God's provision? Of course, you are paid for your work, but who gave you the natural talents and abilities to do it? Who providentially opens the door of opportunity to be at the right place at the right time to find or make a place to work, get a promotion or close a big sale? When the Israelites were about to begin a prosperous life in the "Promised Land" that God had given them, Moses cautioned them, "You may say to yourself, 'My power and the strength of my hands have produced this wealth for me.' But remember the Lord your God, for it is he who gives you the ability to produce wealth..." (Deuteronomy 17–18a)

When you commit yourself to serving God first and submit your will to His, then you can be confident that He will enable you to work in a way that will meet your basic needs without throwing your life out of balance.

One way is to live within your means. If your work pays you an average income or better, a few important adjustments in your lifestyle could enable you to live comfortably on your basic income without putting in extra hours of overtime or taking on a second job. For example, you could sell your house and buy a smaller one with lower monthly payments; buy a late-model used car instead of a new one; eat more meals at home instead of in restaurants; car-pool to work instead of commuting alone or buying a second car.

Paying off credit card debt and then avoiding it is a significant way to increase your spendable income. Every dollar you save on interest is another dollar in your pocket. To add another dollar to your pocket by working for it, you have to earn as much as $1.50 or more to have a dollar left after paying taxes and work-related expenses.

Going to a cash basis, or paying off your credit card balances every month, can increase your spendable income by as much as 50% or more if you are making most of your purchases on credit and paying interest. Truly, that is not an easy thing to do, but neither is it complicated. You simply cut up your credit cards (except for one that you resolve to use only for such things as rental deposits or emergencies) and pay as much as you can spare over the minimum payment every month. Shop for the lowest rates available while you pay down the debt. Take advantage of introductory offers to transfer balances. If possible, consolidate the accounts into one with the lowest rate you can get. Otherwise, increase the amount of monthly payment on the account with the highest rate first, while making minimum payments on the others. When it is paid off, add its monthly payment to the minimum payment of the account with the next highest rate. Be sure to close the accounts as you pay them off and keep only one or two if you want to use revolving charges after you get out of debt. (Credit reporting agencies consider available credit as debt, whether you are using it or not.)

Another option is a consolidation loan from your bank or credit union; but be careful. If you do not stop using your credit cards, a consolidation loan will only put you deeper into debt. You must be committed to simplifying your lifestyle and reducing excessive consumption.

Managing more effectively the income you have can meet some of your financial needs without putting in more hours at work. God may have already provided all the income you need if you practice good stewardship.

On the other hand, you could be underemployed, working long hours just to eke out subsistence income. In that case, you might need to ask God for faith to step out of your familiar "comfort zone" and apply for a better job. If lack of education or job skills is holding you back, then let it be known in your church that you are interested in taking night classes at a local college or job training school. Take the initiative and select the course of study you would like to pursue as if money were no object. Pray about it. Ask others to pray with you. When you commit yourself to a worthwhile endeavor, you might be pleasantly surprised at how many people God inspires to help and encourage you, and the ways He supplies the resources you need to do His will.

Jesus promised that God would provide food and shelter. He did not promise that every believer would be affluent. That is an expectation that comes from American culture. If you are overworking yourself (or holding on to a job that overworks you) in order to own more things, then the things own you, and you are building your life around them instead of Christ. A life centered on Christ will be in balance.

Accept Your Humanity.

> *"A fool's work wearies him; he does not know the way to town." (Ecclesiastes 10:15)*

Solomon said that only a fool would allow his work to wear him down and be ignorant of the obvious problem he creates for himself. Matthew Henry explains, "All their labor is for the world and the body, and the meat that perishes, and in this labor they spend their strength, and exhaust their spirits, and weary themselves for very vanity..." The second phrase in the verse is an idiomatic expression that means one who wearies himself with work is ignorant of what is obvious to everyone else.

We often excuse ourselves for making a mistake by saying, "After all, I'm only human!" Yet we fail to apply that obvious truth when we allow ourselves to be overworked. We plan our schedules as if we have an unlimited supply of energy and stamina. Thinking that we are "getting the most out of life," we consider being over-programmed as normal and healthy. We accept labels that condone this behavior, such as "Super Mom" or "Winner." The fact is we are just human candles that are burning up at both ends. If we do not come to terms with our humanity and find a healthy balance, we will eventually burn out.

One way to achieve balance is to choose carefully the tasks you expect to accomplish each day. Ask yourself, "What difference will it make ten years from now whether I do this activity or not?" If it is necessary to keep your career on track, your marriage intact, maintain a relationship with your family and good friends, remain connected to your church and community, exercise your spiritual gift, or maintain your spiritual, emotional and physical health, then put it on your list. If there will be no significant negative results should it not get done, if it could be done just as well or better by someone else, if it is a selfish indulgence or self aggrandizement, then leave it off your list. Even then you could end up with a lengthy list of worthwhile things to do.

Accepting your human limitations requires choosing between doing what is good and doing what is best. For example, you might have to say "No" to serving on a church committee if you are already involved in a discipleship program that requires a meeting every week. When making up your "To Do" list, remember, it is a human being you are planning for, not a machine. Balance your aspirations for the day with your human limitations.

Limit Your Labor.

"Six days you shall labor and do all your work,
but the seventh day is a Sabbath to the Lord your God.
On it you shall not do any work...
For in six days the Lord made the heavens and the
earth, the sea, and all that is in them, but he rested on
the seventh day." (Exodus 20: 9-11)

This is the fourth of the Ten Commandments God gave to Moses on Mount Sinai. It states a principle that is vital to a balanced life: man needs one day of rest each week. The atheistic Soviet Union experimented with a seven-day work week. They finally abandoned it because it was unproductive. Communist planners discovered that workers' morale and productivity improved dramatically when they were given one day a week to rest. Some Asian societies still adhere to a seven-day work week. The result has been a higher rate of heart attacks and suicide than in Western societies.

Christians have been released from the specific requirements of the Mosaic Law. That is why we worship on the first day of the week, Sunday, instead of the seventh, Saturday, which is the Jewish Sabbath. When we rest from our works and trust in the work of Christ on the cross and His resurrection for our salvation, we experience the fulfillment of the fourth commandment. (See Hebrews 4:1-11.)

Nevertheless, the principle remains true, that all men, including Christians, need one day of rest each week. God rested from His work of creation, not because He was tired, but to set an example for mankind to follow. Not being under the Law of Moses, we have many more options for utilizing that day of rest. As in Moses' time, part of the day should be spent worshipping God in fellowship with other believers. The rest of the day we are free to spend as we see fit. Jesus said, "The Sabbath was made for man, not man for the Sabbath..." (Mark 2:27)

The most important guideline to follow is to engage in activities that are different from what you do the other six days of the week. Spend time with your family. Putter around with your hobby. Enjoy recreational activities. But don't take your play too seriously. Don't work at it or be too competitive or compulsive about it. Remember, the purpose is relaxation and a refreshing change of pace from your regular routine. Plan some time for rest, solitude, silence and meditation.

If you are a pastor or staff worker in a church, Sunday is a workday for you. Take off another day for your "Sabbath."

Adjust Your Values.

"And I saw that all labor and all achievement spring from man's envy of his neighbor." (Ecclesiastes 4:4a)

Ask yourself, "How do I determine what is enough in the area of possessions and creature comforts?" If you do not actively think about it, you will most likely be drawn into the temptation to "keep up with the Joneses." For example, why do you decide you need to buy a new car? Is it because the one you have does not have many miles of useful service left in it? If you faithfully follow the manufacturer's recommendations for maintaining and servicing your car, you can drive a domestic make efficiently for 80,000 to 100,000 miles, and some foreign makes for well over 200,000 miles. Typically, the decision has more to do with the desire to own a new car because friends, relatives or neighbors have bought one.

The unprecedented affluence of the '90s has created extraordinary pressure on the average American to achieve an ever-higher living standard. Have you heard someone who lived through the Great Depression of the 1930s say something like this: "When I was growing up, we didn't have much money to spend; but we didn't consider ourselves to be poor, because most of our friends and family didn't have much money either." In the 21st century, we compare our lifestyles to those of our prosperous friends and family or perhaps to fictional characters depicted in television programs and movies, or even the real "rich and famous" people in the news. If our standard of living does not equal or exceed the standards of the people around us, we feel that we are not keeping up the "winner" image we desire to maintain. That feeling is an important part of the driving force behind the frustrating frenzied push to "get ahead" that we often refer to as "the rat race." "This, too, is meaningless, a chasing after the wind." (Ecclesiastes 4:4b) Somewhere between the austerity of the depression and the "you can have it all" mentality of postmodern society there is a balance point. When we renounce our envious desires, we can adjust our values and find that balance.

> *"Better one handful with tranquility than two handfuls with toil and chasing after the wind."*
> *(Ecclesiastes 4:6)*

Some of the suggestions for lifestyle changes we have made so far might seem a bit radical or too stringent to you. Did you think that going against your culture and restructuring your life to align with biblical values would be easy? We never intended to give you that impression. What we are urging you to consider is that whatever changes you have to make to break out of your excessive busy-ness patterns are worth doing because they help you to become more effective without being frenzied.

One definition of insanity is "repeating the same behavior while expecting different results." If that is what you are doing, then you are out of touch with reality. If you want to achieve balance in your life, then you must be willing to adjust your values and change your behavior. You can do that by deciding to simplify your lifestyle.

There is nothing wrong with an affluent lifestyle if you can afford it. God can use people as witnesses to the gospel in every socio-economic level of society. If you can afford a spacious house, expensive cars, boats, etc., without letting your life get out of balance and compromising biblical priorities, then use those things to the glory of God. But if your lifestyle compels you to work long hours and miss the sleep you need every night, if it interferes with your family and church relationships, if it creates unhealthy stress, if it erodes your spiritual and emotional well-being, then you need to simplify your lifestyle. Sell the big house and buy one with a smaller mortgage that lets you sleep better at night. Trade in the expensive car and buy one with payments that won't strain your budget. If necessary, find a less demanding job that will allow you to have more time at home with your family. Yes, that means lowering your standard of living. But there is wisdom in living on less if that is what frees you to live a more meaningful and purposeful life. You must decide what is most important to you and how far you are willing to go to achieve balance in your life.

"What good is it for a man to gain the whole world, yet forfeit his soul?" (Mark 8:36)

Jesus asks us one of the most significant questions we will ever consider. It cuts through all the confusion and banality of modern living and makes us think about what, after all, is truly, fundamentally important in life. There are basically two competing value systems that define what is most important in life: the way of the world and the way of the cross.

Jesus had just announced to His disciples that He would soon go to Jerusalem where He would suffer rejection and abuse at the hands of the religious leaders, be killed, and then be resurrected three days later. Peter ignored the mention of resurrection and rebuked Jesus for His willingness to die under such circumstances. Jesus responded by rebuking Peter, saying, "You are a stumbling block to me; you do not have in mind the things of God, but the things of men." (Matthew 16:23) Peter was expressing the generally accepted worldly wisdom that one must value his own self-interest and security more than anything else.

Jesus offered Peter and the rest of the disciples another way of deciding what is most important in life—the way of the cross. "If anyone would come after me, he must deny himself and take up his cross and follow me. For whoever wants to save his life will lose it, but whoever loses his life for me will find it." (Matthew 16:24-25)

The cross in the first century meant only one thing—death by execution. It was the "state of the art" instrument for torture and death. Romans considered it so humiliating and horrific that they passed a law protecting all Roman citizens from crucifixion, no matter how heinous their crimes might be. No wonder Peter and the other disciples shrank from Jesus' revelation that to follow Him would lead them to a cross!

Jesus obviously did not mean that every one of His disciples would be required to hang on a Roman cross. What He meant was that every one who follows Him must make a conscious decision to die to himself: to die to self protection at all costs, to selfish ambitions, to self aggrandizement, to worldly standards of self-fulfillment. The true disciple must decide to live for Christ no matter what it may cost him in worldly gain. Human wisdom says that is too much to ask; if you buy into that value system you will be a "loser."

But Jesus asserts that just the opposite is true. Those who adjust their values and dedicate their whole lives and everything they possess and hold dear to serving Christ will be richly rewarded when He returns in glory to establish His kingdom. Those who hold back and try to protect their own self-interests will lose everything.

Jesus proved that His promise will hold true by going to the cross Himself and then rising from the dead three days later. Then He ascended to the place of honor at His Father's right hand. (Acts 2:33) All of the original disciples except Judas chose the way of the cross. Ten of them died violent deaths at the hands of those who opposed their preaching of the Christian message. John was tortured and sentenced to confinement and hard labor in a rock quarry on the Isle of Patmos. Were they losers? Jesus promised, "For the Son of Man is going to come in his Father's glory with his angels, and then he will reward each person according to what he has done." (Matthew 16:27)

Those who choose the way of the world must consider time to be their worst enemy. Eventually it will take everything they are living for away from them. They must work harder, faster and longer to cram everything they ever wanted into one life-time. But in the end, they are just living to die.

When we accept the way of the cross, we die to live. Jesus made another promise: "...I have come that they may have life, and have it to the full." (John 10:10) Only when you are ready to face death can you begin to live life to the fullest degree. The apostle, Paul, said, "For to me to live is Christ and to die is gain." (Philippians 1:21) By adjusting our values to live a life that serves and honors Christ, we can determine what is ultimately most important and offset the "weight of the world" with eternal values.

Nourish Your Inner Life.

"I delight in your decrees. I will not neglect your word." (Psalm 119:16)

For most of each day, we will be exposed to a barrage of words and images that impress on us the values of our culture. We need time every day in the Word of God to counter-balance that influence. In this psalm, David reveals one of the reasons that he became "a man after God's own heart." In his youth, he committed himself to live according to the teachings and commands of God's Word. If you consider reading and studying your Bible as just one more obligatory task that must be added to an already overcrowded schedule, it will probably be the first thing you neglect when you become "too busy." But when you decide to commit your whole life to Christ, to loving and serving Him, then learning more about God and His will for you becomes a delight.

Be honest with yourself. Don't you manage to find time to do most of the things that you truly want to do, the ones that give you the most pleasure in life? David's desire was for communion with God. "I seek you with all my heart; do not let me stray from your commands." (Psalm 119:10) When you make the decision to seek God with all your heart, then finding time for Bible reading and study will be easy for you.

For most people, early morning is the best time. Then you have all day to reflect on what you read. You can always get up a few minutes earlier no matter how crowded your schedule is. (Just be sure to go to bed a few minutes earlier at night to get in your eight hours of sleep.) Some people are nocturnal. They prefer to read their Bible at night when they are settling down to go to sleep. It is not a bad idea to begin and end your day with Bible reading, but don't make a chore out of it. Do it the way that best fits your disposition. Keep it a delight.

> *"...Jesus often withdrew to lonely places and prayed."*
> *(Luke 5:16)*

Jesus was a busy man. As news of His unique teaching and healing ministry spread, crowds of people came to hear Him speak and to seek healing. With several speaking engagements every day, and in between long lines of sick people, each one asking for personal attention and a healing touch, can you imagine the time pressure and stress this created for Jesus? Yet, Luke informs us that during the most hectic phase of His earthly ministry Jesus frequently withdrew from His other responsibilities and spent time in prayer. The busier Jesus became, the more He needed time alone to pray. He always maintained perfect balance between giving out power and strength in work and service, and taking it in through rest and spiritual renewal. Do you dare to assume that you need prayer less than Jesus did? See Chapter 7 for more information about solitude, silence and prayer.

Commit Your Schedule to God.

> *"There is a time and season for everything under*
> *Heaven." (Ecclesiastes 3:1)*

This verse introduces a vivid description of the way the Bible views time and history. It stresses the totality of God's control.

No matter what happens, one way or the other, time moves forward and history unfolds in the way God ordains. It is a cyclical view of time. Yet, other passages in the Bible (such as Matthew 28:20; I Corinthians 15:24; and Revelation 22:13) indicate that history as we know it began at the creation of the universe and is moving toward a goal, namely the Second Coming of Christ. So the biblical view of time is not static, but has a linear aspect. To picture this concept in three dimensions, imagine a spiral moving along a straight line from one end of it to the other.

Man can cause events to happen that affect his experience in time, but history moves forward with a certain inevitability. The worst thing a man can do is attempt to plan and order his life without regard to what God is doing. The best thing he can do is to discern what part of the cycle time is moving through and cooperate with it. That means committing to God the way you spend your time.

If the way you spend your time is out of balance, then most of your life will be out of balance, too. God is not the author of confusion. When you commit your time schedule to Him, He will lead you into order and balance. Chapter 5 will explore this subject in more detail.

Enjoy Each Moment.

> *"That everyone may eat and drink, and find satisfaction in all his toil—this is the gift of God."*
> *(Ecclesiastes 3:13)*

Work was not always toilsome and difficult. When God placed man in the Garden of Eden, He gave him work to do—tending the garden. It did not become toilsome and difficult until after man sinned by disobeying God's command to abstain from eating fruit from the tree that imparted knowledge of good and evil. Part of man's punishment was a curse. "Cursed is the ground because of you; through painful toil you will eat of it all the days of your life." (Genesis 3:17)

Under the curse for man's sin, work is naturally painful. Yet, because of God's mercy and grace, it is still possible to find satisfaction in it. There is honor in labor. Most jobs contribute something useful to human society. If your job doesn't, by all means look for a better one. If you manage a business, you must be providing goods or services that people need, as well as a livelihood for your employees. Airline workers help people visit their families, do their jobs, enjoy vacations, or get medical treatment. Food service workers provide nourishment and enjoyable dining experiences. Retail workers supply clothing, appliances that make life easier, toys for children. Health care workers aid and comfort people who are sick. On and on the list could go. There is satisfaction in serving other people. Furthermore, there is dignity in providing your own living. Even though you don't deserve it, God wants to give you the gift of enjoying your work. Satisfaction in your work balances its pain and difficulty.

"A heart at peace gives life to the body..."
(Proverbs 14:30)

The Bible views man as a whole entity including body, mind and spirit. Whatever is going on in one part of man invariably affects the other two areas. The Hebrews used the word "heart" the way Westerners use the word "mind." When your mind is at peace and relaxed, your body benefits. The opposite is true as well. Most of the things we worry about and stress over either work themselves out to a satisfactory conclusion or don't amount to much in the long run. Only a relatively few things in life are of major importance. We can trust God's grace and providence to deal with them. So, relax! You will be healthier for it.

"Come to me, all you who are weary and burdened and
I will give you rest. Take my yoke upon you and learn
from me, for I am gentle and humble in heart, and you
will find rest for your souls. For my yoke is easy and
my burden is light." (Matthew 11:28-30)

The context of this great invitation is particularly important for its understanding and our discussion of busy-ness. Jesus had just poured out His heart in prayer and praise to God the Father for the way He has chosen to reveal Himself to man. He did not reveal Himself to the "wise and learned." That was a reference to the Scribes and Pharisees, who prided themselves on their mastery of human reason and wisdom, who thought they understood what God is like and what is necessary to know Him. Rather, it was God's "good pleasure" to reveal Himself to "little children." They are the ones who humble themselves and come to Jesus for instruction, for He is the Son of God who alone reveals the Father. Here is a profound revelation: those who want to know the truth about God must surrender their preconceived ideas and allow themselves to be re-educated by Jesus' words and works.

The "wise and learned" postmodern thinkers and teachers of the 21st century have concluded that there is no objective reality, and certainly nothing that can be known about a personal God. Reason no longer applies, so each individual is free to make up his own reality in his head. Language is meaningless except as each individual gives it his own meaning to create the image or the effect he desires. Man is free to create god in his own image, which in the final analysis means that man becomes his own god. We have already explained how this way of thinking drives men to fanatical frenzied activity in their useless efforts to give life meaning and purpose. To break free from the culture of busy-ness, you must give up the postmodern mindset and humbly return to the basic truths about God that secular humanism abandoned during the "Enlightenment."

Jesus says that those truths are found in Him alone. "Come to me," He says. He directs His invitation specifically to "all who are weary and burdened." It is a terrible burden to be your own god. You are responsible for everything! Jesus promises to give you "rest," a word that could be better translated "relief."

Jesus is not offering a life of indolence and ease. Having too much free time makes life boring. Knowing and serving God through devotion to Christ involves responsibilities, even trials and hardship. He invites us to take His yoke and "learn" who He is and what He requires. Jesus Himself "learned" what the will of God for Him required when He went to the cross. "Although he was a son, he learned obedience from what he suffered and, once made perfect, he became the source of eternal salvation for all who obey him…" (Hebrews 5:8) Since He has suffered as a man, Jesus is the ideal teacher: one who is "gentle and humble in heart."

Jesus' requirements of us might seem heavy at times, yet they are easy to bear. He said, "For my yoke is easy and my burden is light." When a farmer living near Nazareth was ready to break in a new team of oxen that had never plowed before, he would take the oxen to the carpenter's shop, probably the one where Jesus worked with His father, Joseph. There the carpenter carefully measured them and custom-made a yoke for them. If the yoke did not fit properly, it would rub sores on the animal's shoulders when it strained at the plow. But if the yoke was "easy," made to fit just right, the ox could plow all day without injury. Jesus, the carpenter's son from Nazareth, knows all about yokes. His yoke fits just right. The tasks He gives you to do are suited to your temperament and spiritual gifts. Because we serve Him out of love, they are never a heavy burden. The word Jesus used for "burden" comes from the word for "cargo" or "load," but He used the diminutive form. "My little burden is light," He said.

When you stop trying to control your life according to your own will and submit to Jesus Christ, "you will find rest." Jesus does not want to add to your misery by increasing your busyness with tasks and responsibilities that you cannot manage. He offers you relief, refreshment for your soul. He offers you a balanced life. Enjoy it!

You might be well into your life's flight, but it is not too late to check your course. Is your life so out of balance that you are not getting at least eight hours of sleep on a regular basis? If so, you could be two degrees off course and heading toward a destination that is many miles away from where you want to go.

WHY THE BIG HURRY?

Another deviation from our flight plan is in the way we spend our waking hours. Americans are increasingly in a hurry. We expect things to happen now, not later, and have little patience with delays. One reason is the improvements in technology. In the 18th century, a man on horseback could travel at a top speed of about twenty miles per hour, and then only for short periods of time. The first automobiles could travel only slightly faster because of the poor road conditions. Now super highways permit travel at speeds up to seventy-five miles per hour. Bullet trains glide on cushions of air and magnetic fields at two hundred miles per hour. Conventional jetliners soar at over five hundred miles per hour.

Most of the daily routines in our lives take only a fraction of the time they used to require. Microwave ovens cook meals in minutes that used to take an hour or two to prepare. Sometimes even that is not fast enough for us, so we eat in "fast food" restaurants where the food is cooked and ready to eat before we walk through the door...or wheel into the drive-through. One national hamburger chain is experimenting in Dallas, Texas, with scanning equipment that can read a code number from a tag in your car and charge your meal to your credit card, saving the time it takes to make change at the "first window."

Business documents sent through the mail require days or even weeks for delivery, but fax machines send them anywhere in the world in just a few minutes. Likewise, an e-mail letter travels to its destination at the speed of light.

There is no need to wait until you get to the office or back to your home to make a telephone call. Most people carry cell phones with them now. When was the last time you took a ride in your car, or went to a ball game and turned off your cell phone? Studies indicate that use of the cell phone is already adding 30 to 45 minutes a day to our week. The constant need for "connection" is in itself a stressor that forces relaxation to take a back seat to "perceived progress."

Fifty years ago when futurists anticipated the development of some of these devices, they predicted that Americans would enjoy more leisure time because of all the time and labor saved. They were dead wrong! Just the opposite has occurred. Instead of expecting to accomplish the same amount of work and responsibility, finishing it in less time, we cram even more work into each day, and take on more responsibilities than we ever would have dared in the past.

PLANET EARTH: AN ALIEN ENVIRONMENT?

We imagine that surely the good we get from technological improvements outweighs the bad ten-to-one. That one negative, however, might in the final analysis destroy the ten good factors. For example, suppose you receive ten positive pieces of mail today. One indicates that you won the sweepstakes for a million dollars. Another informs you that your child who just graduated from high school has been offered a full scholarship to one of the top universities in the nation. The other eight contain similar good news; but the eleventh envelope is from your doctor. He explains that the results of your lab report indicate you have inoperable cancer. Now the other ten letters don't seem as important to you anymore. When we are too busy to live, we cannot enjoy the benefits that technology is supposed to provide.

Instead of providing a life of leisure and luxury, technology is creating an environment that is increasingly alien to the conditions in which the human mind and body were designed to live and flourish. For example, when travel was slower, our bodies had time to adjust to the changes in the environment. But when we jet across several time zones in just a few hours, our biological clocks do not have time to re-set. The result is a sickness called "jet lag" that is familiar to experienced travelers.

Jet lag is not a serious ailment, and it goes away after a day of rest and recuperation. But what about similar problems that occur nearly every day of our lives without remedy? The human mind and emotions are not like our machines that function constantly and efficiently without interruption. Rather, they naturally work in cycles of activity and inactivity. The mind needs time to reflect and process the information that is streaming into it every day. The emotions need a down cycle to calm them from the myriad of stimuli encountered during the day. When we do not allow this down time to occur, our bodies begin to get sick.

Dr. Archibald D. Hart, dean of the Graduate School of Psychology at Fuller Theological Seminary, warns that unrelenting stress produces excessive levels of adrenaline in the bloodstream that eventually can become the underlying cause of heart disease as well as other ailments. Some degree of stress is desirable, he explains. The release of adrenaline it stimulates gives us energy to deal with the challenges of life and sharpens our mental acuity. Without it we would be rather dull and listless much of the time.

But the body needs time following a stressful experience to process the extra adrenaline. Even positive experiences like being commended by your employer, attending a concert, watching a suspenseful or action adventure movie, or even attending a high energy contemporary worship service can produce stress. When your days and evenings consist of one stressful experience after another with no letup, the adrenaline in your bloodstream remains at high enough levels to cause physical damage and burnout. Some of the symptoms are headaches, ulcers, muscle spasms and digestive problems.[3]

STEER CLEAR OF STRESS.

To avoid disease brought on by stress, give yourself permission to relax and unwind several times during the day. Instead of consuming a caffeine drink on your "coffee break" (which stimulates the adrenal glands), try a couple of relaxation exercises that the authors recommend for times when you feel "keyed up."

Breathing Exercise

1. Sit in a chair or lie down in a quiet area.

2. Take a deep breath and hold it, counting as long as you can—1,001,…1,002,…1,003,…

3. While you are counting, squeeze your hands as tight as you can.

4. When you feel you are about to burst, let the air out of your lungs slowly and relax your hands.

5. After all the air is out, breathe deeply—don't allow yourself to gasp for air.

6. Take several slow deep breaths and then hold your breath again, repeating the counting process. If you are beginning to relax, you will be able to count to a higher number. (Your body needs more oxygen when under stress, so when you're relaxed there is less need for oxygen and you should be able to increase the count.)

Muscle Relaxation

Muscle relaxation exercises are similar to the natural body response that often accompanies a yawn. Specific muscles contract and tense up, then release and relax.

To begin, settle back as comfortably as you can. Let all your muscles go loose and heavy. Wrinkle up your forehead...wrinkle it tighter...then stop wrinkling it...relax and smooth it out. Now tense up your right shoulder...contract the muscles even tighter...now relax.

Starting at the top of your body and working your way down, continue to isolate different muscle groups. Follow the same process of tensing and relaxing each one. Try to achieve deeper and deeper levels of relaxation.

• • •

Any time you feel stressed, you can use these relaxation techniques to help control your feelings and their physical signs (such as sweating, higher pulse, or tightening in the chest). When those tensions occur, take time to break the pressure cycle. Push back and breathe deeply or get up and walk around for a few minutes.

If you need help unwinding, you might also find it relaxing and therapeutic to work with your hands, complete routine chores, or listen to restful music. It's not by accident that people say, "peace and quiet" in the same breath. Noise and confusion contribute to stress, so if at all possible, schedule periods of quiet and solitude in your day.

Perhaps the best way to relieve stress and lower adrenaline levels is to exercise. Almost any kind of exercise you choose will be beneficial. Cassie Findley believes that the best exercise is one you enjoy doing. It helps to clean out your system, promotes relaxation, and builds up your serotonin level. (Serotonin is a neurotransmitter that positively affects many behavior patterns, including mood, learning and sleep.) In fact, research among AIDS patients found that the one thing that often put AIDS into remission was exercise. Twenty to thirty minutes of aerobic exercise at least three times a week would be ideal. But it is not an all-or-nothing benefit package. Walking or any increase in physical activity can help. Try parking farther from your office and walking the distance, using the stairs instead of the elevator, or taking a brisk walk around the block during your lunch hour. Improvise. Learn to look for opportunities to be active.

CHECK YOUR COURSE HEADING.

These recommendations require some significant changes in your lifestyle; and changes are hard to make. Dr. Shad Helmstetter, author of *Choices,* wrote, "It is only when you exercise your right to *choose* that you can also exercise your right to *change.*"[4] Check your life course heading. If you are always in a hurry, choose to slow down and give yourself permission to relax.

By now you may realize that your life is off-course. If you are a young adult or a new Christian, you might be able to make a course correction and continue with your flight plan. On the other hand, if you have been on the wrong course heading for many years, it might be too late for a mere course correction. It is even possible that you filed the wrong flight plan because you have never made the decision to trust Christ for salvation. When it is too late for a course correction, the best action is to swallow your pride, admit that you are headed the wrong way in your life, turn around and go back to a new starting point. The Bible calls that decision "repentance." Change your mind about the way you have been living. Decide that you will no longer let the culture dictate how you live your life. Accept Christ's invitation to receive His yoke; yield your will to His will. Trust Him to forgive you and to guide you into the abundant, balanced life that He promised.

CHAPTER 3

The Little Children Suffer

ALONG FOR THE RIDE

At 5:30 A.M. John and Karen's clock radio begins to blare soft rock music. Time to start another typical day. By 6:00 they have dressed in time to wake up Amy, their seven year-old daughter, and Josh, their fifteen year-old son. They have to leave early today for Amy's 7:30 A.M. piano lesson. (It used to be on Friday after school, but Amy was having trouble concentrating; so her teacher suggested early Tuesday morning when she is not so tired.)

As John keeps the kids moving, Karen brews the coffee, sets out the children's breakfasts, empties the dishwasher and packs Amy's lunch. At 6:30 she and John wolf down a bagel with coffee just before the children enter the kitchen for their breakfast "blitz."

John has to go straight to his office for an early staff meeting, so Karen loads the children into the Explorer and drops Amy off at her piano lesson. She has just enough time to drive Josh to his high school, fill the car with gas, and double back for Amy. Then she drives to Amy's elementary school where Karen teaches third grade.

After school, Karen rushes to the high school to pick up Josh and drive him to his soccer game at 4:30. When she isn't cheering for Josh she is on her cell phone coordinating her schedule with John. He needs to work late, so Karen will have to drive Josh to the church youth meeting at 7:00 tonight.

When the game ends, Karen and the kids eat supper at McDonald's, drive home for Josh to shower and dress, then leave for church. Returning at about 7:20, Karen insists that Amy perform the practice exercises her piano teacher assigned.

John arrives at 8:00. He has just enough time to make and eat a sandwich for his supper before it is time to pick up Josh at church. They return at 9:00. John helps Josh with his homework till 10:00 while Karen goes through Amy's bedtime routine, then washes clothes and tidies up the house. While Karen grades papers from 10:00 to 11:00, Josh does internet research for a term paper under his father's supervision. (John wants to make sure that Josh develops the skills he will need to excel at the "ivy league" university he has picked out for him.)

At 11:00 they start their bedtime routines. They will all need the rest. Josh has another soccer game tomorrow and a karate lesson afterwards. Amy goes to children's choir practice at church.

• • • •

The above example is fictitious, but it is a composite based on documented cases of real families. In fact, some of the actual experiences were even more extreme than this example. Not only are adults caught up in the culture of busy-ness, but they are also taking their children with them for the ride. Parents and their children seem to be running a marathon race with no finish line in sight. The process of raising children has in itself become a major factor in the cycle of excessive busy-ness. Most parents only want what is best for their children, but the time has come to ask, "Are the children better off for parents' efforts on their behalf?"

Child raising has not always been this way. What happened? How did we get where we are now? Many baby boomers have delightful memories of a rather freewheeling childhood. Their parents' main concern each day was that they come home in time for dinner when the whole family gathered around the table for a wholesome meal and conversation. When not in school, a child spent much of his time riding his bicycle to a friend's house to play, climbing trees, making a clubhouse out of a refrigerator carton, enjoying an unsupervised game of sandlot softball or shooting hoops in a neighbor's driveway. Children having experiences like that in 21st century America are considered to be "deprived."

"Beep-beep"

The first inkling of change began on October 4, 1957. Americans were shocked and chagrined when Soviet Russia successfully launched Sputnik I, the first man-made satellite to orbit the earth. Broadcasting on a common radio frequency, its "beep-beep" was literally heard around the world. A month later, Sputnik II blasted Leika, the dog, into earth orbit and monitored its vital signs for a week. Americans resented a communist country taking the lead from them in what came to be known as the "space race." Politicians began to criticize the American school system for "falling behind" the Russian education system, especially in the disciplines of math and science. There was a rush of students to enroll in physics and science courses, and all educators felt under pressure to be more effective.

Burn, baby, burn!

Perhaps as a reaction to the tightening of discipline in schools and colleges, revolution-oriented students during the turbulent '60s and '70s demanded that the education system become more student centered, diverse, nonconformist, and creative. Destructive demonstrations and even the besieging of a few college presidents in their offices convinced educators to cooperate. Colleges introduced new elective courses emphasizing cultural diversity and similar courses not related to traditional academic disciplines. Even grammar schools began to assign less homework. By 1981 students in the first through third grades were averaging about fifty-two minutes of homework per week.[1]

BACK TO BASICS

Then, on April 26, 1983, the pendulum began to swing in the opposite direction. Terrel Bell, President Ronald Reagan's Secretary of Education, released a report he had commissioned titled, "A Nation at Risk." It repudiated the revolutions imposed on education in the '60s and '70s and challenged American educators to go "back to basics." The time had come, it stated, to assert authority again and put order back into schools. The effect on education was electrifying. By 1997, first through third graders were averaging over two hours of homework per week, twice as much as in the early '80s. Math and science requirements for high school graduation also doubled, and the average school day lengthened.[2]

GUILTY PARENTS

In addition to this trend in the education system, parents began to program more activities for their children outside of the school classroom. One motivation that causes parents to overprogram their children is guilt. Maintaining an affluent lifestyle these days usually takes two incomes. In 1975, only 44% of mothers worked outside the home. By 1985 the figure rose to 54%, and in 1999 it reached 62%. Dr. Joshua Sparrow of Boston's Children's Hospital says that parents feel they are not spending enough time with their children.[3] So, when parents spend time with their children they feel pressured to "make it count," to do something practically every minute that will contribute to the child's future success.

DRIVEN BABIES

Unfortunately, these guilt-ridden parents have been sold the idea that the process of conditioning their child's mind for intellectual achievement begins in the earliest stages of infancy. The most extreme example is a company that markets handheld "tummy speakers" designed to stimulate the baby's growing brain with music and voice messages while he is still in his mother's womb.

The underlying assumption is the theory that there is a "window of opportunity" for learning certain skills during a child's development. If a parent fails to provide the right stimulation at the right time, then the child supposedly will never "catch up" to the level of achievement attained by other children in his generation who had this advantage. The concern is not just that the child will not measure up to his full potential as an individual, but that he will not be a "winner" in a competitive postmodern culture.

This notion started in 1994 with a report by the Carnegie Corporation. They warned that when both parents pursue careers, their children's needs for intellectual stimulation might not be fulfilled. Their main focus was on school-age children, but two paragraphs buried in the report suggested that the problem could begin in infancy. The media picked up the story, the Head Start program touted it, and eventually the White House organized a conference on childhood development. Working parents across the country feared that their "neglect" had already damaged their children.[4]

To compensate, parents began to buy a spate of products designed to stimulate children's minds. Playing video tapes of shapes and colors set to Mozart's music, parents are told, can jump start a child's readiness for kindergarten and even enhance his ability to do math. A survey of parents with a high school education or less by a nonprofit research organization called Zero to Three determined that 80% of them were busily using flash cards, television and computer games to engage their babies' minds.[5]

THE "WINDOW OF OPPORTUNITY" MYTH

But is this effort to pump up children's IQ's effective or even desirable? In fact, the underlying presupposition is questionable. Promoters of the "window of opportunity" theory frequently refer to the "latest brain research" to support their views and social programs based upon them. Undeniably, many important processes occur during a baby's first three years of development, but Dr. John T. Bruer, a neuroscientist, challenges the idea that brain development during the first three years of life determines how the brain will function for the rest of the individual's life. He also questions the validity of contrived efforts to stimulate the infant's brain in order to raise his IQ. According to Dr. Bruer in his book, *The Myth of the First Three Years*, there is no neuroscience research that supports the critical period, deterministic theory of child development. The small amount of research that has been done in this area either does not support the theory or actually disproves it.

EXUBERANT SYNAPSES

There are three areas of research on which determinists base their theory. One involves studies beginning in the 1970s on the formation of synapses affecting visual functions in early development of animals with highly developed nervous systems, mainly cats and monkeys. (Synapses are the microscopic gaps between nerve endings that serve as paths for the routing of electric impulses in the brain.) In the 1980s research extended to humans and included other areas of brain function.

Peter Huttenlocher and other researchers at the University of Chicago observed that the human brain, like the brains of animals studied earlier, goes through a period of rapid synapse formation in the early stage of development: between birth and one year for humans. At about two years, the synaptic density in the frontal cortex peaks at 50% above the average adult level.[6] Determinists seized this part of the research and drew three conclusions from it.

First, they assumed this must be a critical period because it is the time when most synapses are formed. Then they further assumed that there is a linear relationship between the number of synapses and intelligence. In other words, the babies with the most synapses are the smartest babies.

Second, they claimed that stimulation from the infant's environment cause the synapses to form. Hillary Clinton makes this point in her book, *It Takes a Village.*[7]

Finally, they conclude that this period of rapid synapse formation is the time when basic learning skills are permanently determined. After three years, the process ends, and the brain is set in a pattern.

The problem with these conclusions and assumptions is that they either do not take into account the rest of the body of neurological research that is available, or they misinterpret its meaning. After the initial rapid formation stage, the level of synapses reaches a plateau that lasts from two to sixteen years, the variation occurring in different areas of the brain.[8] There is no neat cut-off point at three years. After that, the number of synapses normally decreases to the average adult level.

None of the research showed any correlation between the number of synapses and superior intelligence. In fact, some of the case studies of fragile-X syndrome, a form of mental retardation, revealed a higher than normal level of synaptic density in the victims' brains. The implication is that the abnormal brain stopped developing at an early stage when the number of synapses was still high. The extra synapses did not result in greater intelligence, but retardation instead. Evidently, the sorting and elimination of unused synaptic connections is a normal part of healthy brain development. Their elimination results in more efficient brain function and greater intellectual capacity.[9]

An analogy would be the files in a personal computer. As a computer is used over time, unused and temporary files accumulate on the hard disk. If they are not deleted periodically, the computer becomes less efficient. Every time it performs a function, it has to sort through the unused files to determine if they contain information the computer needs to perform that function. Eventually, the disk becomes full and cannot store or process any new information.

The research also contradicts the assumption that stimulation from the environment causes the formation of synapses. Rather, the formation of synapses in early development is caused by genetic programming. Goldman-Rakic, a leading neuroscience researcher, informed attendees of a meeting in Denver sponsored by the Education Commission of the States that most learning takes place *after* the stabilization of synaptic formation.[10] The evidence indicates that rapid synaptic formation is a precursor and a preparation for learning experiences, not the other way around as the myth supposes.

Fortunately, the assumption that learning skills are permanently determined by the age of three is also false. A series of studies by Goldman-Racik and Adele Diamond, a developmental psychologist, tested both monkeys and humans for improvement in delayed response tasks. They concluded that certain skills and behaviors first appear in a rudimentary form shortly after the synaptic level peaks occur.[11] Further studies confirmed that these skills continue to develop and improve for many years after the end of rapid synapse formation, extending into adolescence and adulthood. The brain research results clearly indicate that the brain does not become "hard wired" at three years. Rather, it remains flexible and adaptable into adulthood.[12]

Admittedly, there does seem to be a critical period for learning a first language. Deprived "feral" children who grew up without normal human social contact could not master vocabulary and grammar if they were not exposed to a language before puberty, about 12 or 13 years of age. On the other hand, an abused child named Isabelle was not exposed to human language until age 6. She developed a vocabulary of several thousand words and was able to understand complex constructions of grammar.[13] So, there does seem to be a window of opportunity for developing a first language that ends somewhere between 6 and 13 years—not 3.

BLIND KITTENS

Research that tugs the heartstrings of parents, especially mothers, is the study by Nobel Prize winners David Hubel and Torsten Wiesel. They sealed one eye of a newborn kitten. Otherwise, the kitten grew and developed normally. After a few months, they allowed the eye to open. They discovered that, even though the eye was perfectly formed optically, it was blind. The conclusion they drew was that the eye had not connected to the brain neurologically. All the connections to the brain had been used up by the other eye because it was the only one sending stimuli to the brain.[14]

Proponents of the myth have used this research extensively because it seems to validate their beliefs about critical periods of development and because of its emotional impact on parents. When parents are warned that their children could be "damaged" during the first three years if they do not receive enough of the right stimulation, the image of a half-blind kitten fumbling with a ball of yarn sends them scurrying to the store to buy a Mozart video or makes them willing and eager to support any program that offers to help avoid such a plight for their child.

Again, the research does not support these concerns. Other studies done on monkeys have demonstrated that the amount of stimulation is not as important as the pattern of stimulation. Hubel, Wiesel and their colleague, Simon LeVay sealed both eyes of some monkeys from birth to six months. When their eyes were opened for the first time, the monkeys had normal vision in both eyes. No stimulation was necessary for their eyesight to develop normally. Since both eyes were deprived of stimulation, the pattern of stimulation (or lack of it) remained in balance.[15]

Incidentally, there has been much confusion about what is called the "Mozart effect" and babies. Since 1995, many products have been sold to parents with the suggestion that research has proven babies will be smarter if they are stimulated during their development by listening to classical music.

Researchers have observed that playing background music can have a beneficial effect on the listener's spatial skills. In the year 2000, Harvard University released the results of a study called "Project Zero" that compiled the available research on this idea from the last 50 years. The conclusion was that college students scored better on spatial tests using paper and pencil when they listened to background music. However, the effect of the music was temporary and faded away after 15 minutes. There was no evidence that the music had any lasting effect on brainpower or improvement in artistic skills.[16]

Another study observed that preschoolers who took piano lessons experienced an improvement in spatial reasoning skills that lasted for several hours. Note that none of these studies involved infants, and the results in all cases showed no lasting effects. The fact is, there has been no research, and there is no evidence to support the claim that listening to classical CDs or any other kind makes a lasting improvement on babies' spatial or reasoning skills.[17]

On the other hand, there could be some benefit from playing the videos and CDs for babies. Mozart's music, for example, is soothing for most babies; and exposing children to good quality music and art at an early age might lay a foundation for their appreciation of them later in life. That is a beneficial effect; but parents who imagine that the music is improving their baby's brain may be just kidding themselves.

Some parents might object, asserting that they have proven these methods work by teaching their baby to read by age three. They credit themselves for managing his education just right: exposing the child to music, letters and words at precisely the right times to stimulate his developing brain. Actually, they just got lucky and had a child who has a knack for language skill. Every individual child develops skills at his own rate: some faster, and some a little slower.[18]

RAT PLAYGROUNDS

Another pillar of the "window of opportunity" myth is a research experiment with rats. A growing body of evidence has suggested that the environment of lab rats could have an impact on their brain development. In the 1970s Bill Greenough and Fred Volkmar measured the dendritic areas in the brains of lab rats in three groups. The "isolated environment" rats were kept alone in a cage. The "social environment" rats lived together in the same cage. A third group, the "complex environment" rats lived in larger room-like enclosures with other rats. In addition, this group enjoyed obstacles to climb, treadmills to run in, and various toys to play with. The scientists even changed the toys frequently to keep the rats from getting bored. At the end of the experiment, the researchers dissected the rats' brains. The brains of the "complex" rats had about 20% more dendritic area than the brains of the "isolated" rats. Also, the "complex" rats navigated mazes more rapidly, and learned with fewer errors.[19]

The myth literature picked up on this research and touted it as proof positive that "the first three years last forever." Parents and caregivers were assured that the environment they create for their infants and young children will determine how their brains develop for good or ill for the rest of their lives. Subtly, they changed the scientists' term "complex" to "enriched." That gives the impression that parents can actually improve the brain's development by providing more stimulating experiences for their children.

A careful examination of Greenough's experiments raises serious questions about this conclusion. First, the only area of rat brains that seemed to be affected by the experiment was the visual area. There was no measurable difference in any other parts of the rat brains. Furthermore, neuroscientists do not agree among themselves as to whether this rodent research is applicable to brain research for humans and if so, how. Also, use of the term "enriched environment" is misleading. Scientists used the more accurate term "complex environment" because the base line for comparison was the isolated rat in a laboratory cage. Rats living in an urban back alley or under a rural corncrib would have even "richer" experiences, and they would be normal for rats. What the experiments proved was that rats in an abnormal, deprived environment in a laboratory cage do not develop normal healthy brains compared to rats living in an environment that is more like their natural habitat. Environment does make a difference in brain development, but only when it deviates significantly from what is normal and results in extreme deprivation of normal experiences. The experiment proved the effects of deprivation, not "enrichment."

Finally, the experiment actually refuted one of the myth's basic assumptions: that the first three years are a critical period after which synaptic connections cannot be established. The rats used in the experiments varied in age from just-weaned young rats to rats well past their middle age. While the younger rats were more adaptive than the older ones, even the old rats were able to form new synapse connections.[20]

THE TRUE FOUNDATION FOR LEARNING

Parents who busy themselves trying to "build" their young child's brain by providing extra stimulation and cramming learning experiences into the first three years as if that were the only time critical learning skills can be formed may be creating some of the problems they are trying so hard to avoid. If the parents are anxious about their child's learning, they will communicate that anxiety to the child. In addition, children under parental pressure to learn before they are ready will become stressed. If the stress and anxiety continue long enough, the child's learning will be impaired.

Playing videos and CDs featuring shapes and classical music for infants and young children as well as showing flash cards might be beneficial. However, they can deprive a child of essential experiences if they are substituted for personal interaction with parents. The expressions on a mother or father's face, the sound of their voices, being held and cuddled or played with mean more to babies and young children than all the contrived shapes, notes and numbers in a sterile media-learning tool. In the early years, the most important foundation for learning is human bonding, and relationships of trust and respect.[21]

DIVINE WISDOM AND HUMAN COMMON SENSE

The psalmist wrote, "I praise you because I am fearfully and wonderfully made; your works are wonderful, I know that full well." (Psalm 139:14) God in His infinite wisdom created the brain to develop in a way that interacts with its environment. That allows for great flexibility and the ability to adapt to varying conditions. The brain's basic, essential needs for stimulation are such that they inevitably will be met in any semblance of normal experience. For example, practically any environment besides a dark closet will provide varying shades and shapes of light and darkness for an infant's developing eyesight. Unless a baby is abandoned on a remote mountainside, he will inevitably hear the sounds of a parent or some other caregiver's voice with its language patterns, and feel tender caresses when held in their arms. Only in cases of deprivation and abuse will normal healthy development be affected.

Parents need not stress over their imagined responsibility to provide the necessary stimulation for brain development. "Brain building" by parents is neither possible nor desirable. All parents must do is use their God-given common sense and do the things they instinctively know to do. They just need to relax with their baby and enjoy the time they spend together. The most important things parents can do during the first three years is to encourage their baby to form warm relationships with them and others, and to teach them to obey. When addressing the relationship between children and parents, the apostle, Paul, stressed the importance of obedience. "Children, obey your parents in the Lord, for this is right." (Ephesians 6:1) Children who obey their parents will be able to follow instructions when they go to kindergarten and later to school. That is the single most important readiness skill for their future education and mental development.

Even after the determinists have made their case for a critical period in the first three years, the only practical advice they have been able to offer parents has been suggestions such as, "Read to your child. Spend time talking and playing with your child." That is what good parents already knew instinctively that they should do. The best thing parents can do is put down the "brain toys" and pick up their children.

CHILDREN WITH NO CHILDHOOD

Another motivation that causes parents to over-program their children is ambition. Some parents in the middle and upper-middle social classes are driven by ambition, not only for themselves, but also for their children. Their culture has taught them to desire to "be a winner" and "have it all." Since they love their children, they want the same things for them that they want for themselves.

But attaining the previous generation's prosperity is becoming more difficult. Since "baby boomers" are so numerous, the number of their grandchildren who will eventually seek higher education is relatively large, even after being limited by birth control and abortion. In addition, since the "equal rights" legislation passed in the '60s as an outgrowth of the civil rights movement, the top colleges and universities are not as discriminatory in their admission policies. Just being a member of an elite social class no longer gives a prospective student an advantage. He must compete with a growing number of highly motivated other applicants.[22] Aspiring parents anticipating what will look good on a college admission application are programming their children's lives. Childhood has been squeezed out by a curriculum, and play has been replaced by purpose.

PLAY: ANOTHER FOUR-LETTER WORD

Postmodern American culture does not value time children spend in play. A study of school age children by the University of Michigan revealed that the amount of free time—not counting sleeping, eating, studying and participating in organized activities—dropped from 40% in 1981 to 25% in 1997. "See Dick run?" the old readers used to say. These days, many parents would rather for Dick to sit at his desk and study so he can make it into Harvard.[23] They would be gratified to know that recess is being phased out of hundreds of elementary schools. The Atlanta school system has eliminated them already, and many other districts are considering similar measures.[24]

This bias against play for children supposes that the time can be better spent in more productive pursuits. But Stuart Brown, a psychiatrist who founded the Institute for Play in Carmel Valley, California, warns that depriving children of play can result in depression, hostility and the loss of qualities that make us true human beings.[25] Alan Rosenfeld suggests an even more important reason why children need time to play on their own. When a child has time alone, he can dream, fantasize and reflect on things that are important to him. In those moments, the child learns to be at peace with himself, an accomplishment that may have eluded his postmodern parents.[26]

YOUTH SPORTS RUN AMUCK

Postmodern culture is taking its toll on children's organized sports. Although the number of children enrolled in sports programs has grown exponentially in the last ten years, the current dropout rate is estimated to be 70%. The primary reason is the super-aggressive "winner" mentality of the parents and coaches.

Parents are thrusting their children into organized sports before they are old enough to develop an interest—in some cases as early as 3 years old. The expectation, or fear, is that other children will get ahead of them if they don't start early and they will never be able to "catch up."

Actually, there is no basis for those fears. As we mentioned earlier, children tend to develop at their own pace in a set sequence of learning experiences. There is little a parent can do to speed up the process. Starting a child too early in a sport before he is developmentally ready for it can frustrate and discourage him. Once a child has reached his readiness stage, progress can be rapid, and he can easily make up for "lost time."

The result of starting too early is a dramatic increase in injuries. Children's bodies are simply not mature enough or strong enough to sustain the rigorous physical training and demanding play schedules.

Another problem is burnout. If a child is good at a particular sport, his coach is likely to insist that he play and practice year-round for it, even if the child is active in other sports. Particularly difficult is the travel schedule. An away-from-home game can take an entire weekend. Some children play in as many as 135 out-of-town baseball games a year by the age of 12 years. It is not uncommon for a child to play up to 100 soccer games a year by the time she reaches high school. By that time, most of the kids have lost interest in sports because they are simply worn out with them.[27] Worst of all, parents have robbed their children of the fun they should be having when they *play* a sport. After all, that is what it is supposed to be, not another source of stress that uses up most of their free time.

THE PERFECT CHILDHOOD

Postmodern culture presupposes that the past does not matter. There are no lessons to be learned from previous experiences and the older generation's way of doing things. You live in the "now" and shape your own reality the way you want it to be. When this notion is applied to parenting, the result is often a disparaging of the way young adults were raised by their own parents. They imagine that they could have had a perfect childhood if only their parents had "done things right." Modern parents are determined to provide that perfect childhood for their children that they never had themselves.

Hopefully, the primary motivation of these parents is love for their children; but, honestly, it is often the narcissistic desire to live vicariously through their children. They see themselves in their children and want to experience through them the childhood they always wanted but never had.

The problem with this approach to parenting is that nothing can be left to chance or a child's whims if perfection is the goal. Parents must manage every detail of their child's life if it is going to turn out "right." This is a colossal undertaking that will keep parents incredibly busy for as long as their children are in the home. It also keeps the children busy, because there is always another activity that can be scheduled into whatever free time they have that will make their lives "better," and bring them closer to that perfect childhood experience.

What is worse, this striving for perfection obliterates all sense of proportion and sensible priorities. Everything is important; every minute counts. Every mistake is a failure; every failure is a disaster. Every moment that is not filled with programmed activity is lost time and a missed opportunity.

SMOOTH PATH OR SLIPPERY SLOPE?

Parents who set out to plan every detail of their children's lives feel a responsibility to create a smooth path for them to follow. For example, a conscientious mom will not only schedule play dates for her six-year-old son and his friends, but will also decide in advance what activities they will "enjoy." After all, she can't risk her son being disappointed in the experience. That might be detrimental to his social development.

Does a child have a problem? Not to worry, Mom or Dad will take care of it. A ten-year-old daughter receives a "C" grade on a test. Mom calls the teacher. Perhaps she did not make the assignments clear enough or did not review the material with the children sufficiently before the test. "Susie really deserves a grade adjustment or a re-test on the material," she insists.

A twelve-year-old son is assigned to play left field on his little league baseball team; but that is not the position he wants to play. Dad calls the coach. "If you would make Johnny a first baseman or a short-stop, you would have a better team," he suggests... "Just a little friendly advice."

On the surface, it seems that these parents are showing concern for their children's well being. However, there is a downside to shielding children from all the bumps in the road of life. Trying something difficult, making mistakes, failing, learning from the mistakes and trying again is a vital part of the process of growing into responsible adulthood.

Susie would have been better off in the long run if her mother had encouraged her to ask her teacher for an extra assignment to pull up the grade and for some study tips to help prepare for the next test. Johnny could have confronted the coach himself and asked why he did not choose him for short-stop. Then he could have asked the coach to help him develop his catching and throwing skills to the level necessary to be a good shortstop.

No single experience is likely to define the child's whole life. Life is made up of many thousands of events. Failure in one or even several of them does not mean that the child's life will end in failure. Failures can actually help the child discover where his strengths and weaknesses lie. He needs the freedom to experiment with many different interests, and that means the freedom to fail. When parents circumvent the possibility of failure, the child loses the freedom to discover the interests that ignite his passion.

Handling a child's problems for him suggests to the child that he is incompetent to deal with them himself. Children who learn to depend on their parents to solve all their problems will not develop the self-confidence they need to handle problems on their own when they become adults.

A GENERATION OF WORKAHOLICS

The impact of this kind of parenting on the next generation of adults can be seen in a sampling of college students at Princeton University conducted by David Brooks. The first thing that struck Brooks was how busy the students were. For example, he sent e-mail invitations to several dozen students to meet with him in small groups. To his surprise, most of the responses came into his "Inbox" between the hours of 1:55 to 3:23 A.M. When he asked the students, "When do you sleep?" a typical response was, "From 2:00 to 7:00 A.M." Their days and nights were filled with activities: athletic practice at daybreak, morning classes, dorm supervisor duty, lunch, study groups, afternoon classes, volunteer social work, choir practice, dinner, library, science lab, prayer time, exercise workout, and finally, more study into the wee hours of the night. One student admitted that he had to schedule time just to have a conversation with some of his friends. Few of the students took time to go out on dates. They would attend a party every now and then, but they generally agreed that they just did not have time or energy for serious personal relationships.[28]

Brooks noted that none of the students seemed to resent being subjected to excessive demands on their time. Apparently, the students were so accustomed to having every waking hour programmed by their parents and every day overloaded with activities that this workaholic schedule seemed perfectly normal to them.

A GENERATION OF WIMPS

Even more disturbing was Brooks' observation that, compared to the "baby boom" generation, the students were quite compliant and submissive to authority, lacking in passion for social change or justice. Most students did not even have the time to read a newspaper, let alone formulate an opinion about current events. They were content to be told what to do and even what to think so that they could complete their degree requirements and qualify themselves for the best jobs with the biggest salaries. Also missing was concern for developing character and desire to struggle against evil in themselves and society, concepts that used to be the theme of campus life.[29]

It is understandable that these students accept "political correctness" without question, considering the way they were raised by "hyper-parents," who took their authority to an extreme. Parental authority sheltered them from the pitfalls and problems of life, so there was no need to struggle with anything. Parental authority knew what was in their best interest long before they were mature enough to think about it. Parental authority programmed their lives for success. For example, when Cassie Findley was teaching a class at Baylor University, she asked her students what role their parents currently played in their lives. One student replied that her father had planned all four years of her college courses to maximize her college experience and to ensure that she would be competitive when she applied to enter medical school. Another student said that her mother had helped her plan nearly every aspect of her life. If the parents are helping to achieve goals their children have freely chosen, such heavy involvement could be constructive. However, if the children are being programmed to follow a life course designed primarily to satisfy their parents' desires and ambitions, the result could be negative.

By the time they reach college, this generation assumes that the key to success and a good life is to conform to the rules and do what those in authority expect them to do.[30] Have parents who busied themselves to program their children to be "winners" produced a generation of wimps? Time will tell.

A GENERATION OF RADICALS

Not all children are so compliant that they will allow their parents to steal their identity and shape them into reflections of themselves. Parents are taking a terrible risk when they attempt to micro-manage their children's lives. If a child has a strong personality and will, she will insist on expressing her own individuality. The way to do that is to resist or even reject parental authority. The child will be torn between two desires: to please her parents or to express her own personhood. There will be a perpetual duel between the child and the parents, culminating in adolescence, and then extending into adulthood. The child's life will be defined by either conforming to the parents' wishes or rebelling against them as he gravitates to one radical position after another.[31]

BALANCED PARENTING: THE SOLUTION FOR BUSY-NESS

Parents who attempt to create the perfect childhood for their children are almost certain to be disappointed. Their nearly frantic efforts actually create some of the problems they are trying to avoid as well as others that they do not anticipate.

Our Creator has designed babies to develop robust, inquisitive minds with the stimulation that is abundant in even the simplest normal human family environment. It is worse than useless for parents to stress themselves and spend time "enriching" their baby's brain with flash cards and media tools that could be better spent playing, cuddling or reading with the child. What babies need most in the first three years are not contrived methods of brain stimulation, but the development of warm human relationships, social skills and respect for parental authority.

Wise parents will try to find a balance for their children between preparing for adulthood and enjoying the freedom of childhood. Parents have a responsibility to teach their children to be industrious and competent to care for their own basic needs. Good parents insist that their children do their homework and encourage them to develop skills in music, art, and athletics. But children need time to play and enjoy childhood before they take on the stresses and responsibilities of adulthood. Even a little boredom can be good for them. Bored children often become creative in devising ways to fill their time. Over-scheduling children creates the same kinds of stress-related problems their parents are experiencing, and interferes with their learning and emotional development.

Parents must find a balance point between neglect and hyper-parenting. It is good for children to take lessons in music, dancing, karate, art, skating, but not if they do too many of them at the same time. It is good for a child to be involved in team sports, but not if the rest of her free time is already committed to several other activities. It is good to plan ahead for a child's college education, but not if it means sacrificing his childhood and individual personhood for it.

Parents need to use good judgment and set some reasonable limits on their children's activities. They must guide their children to establish priorities in the use of their time. They need to learn when to exert parental authority and when to "back off" and let the child live his own life, make his own decisions, accept responsibility for his failures. They must resist the narcissistic tendency in our culture to live vicariously through their children. If they don't, they will probably raise either a generation of emotionally flat workaholics or passionate angry radicals.[32]

CHAPTER 4

Honey, Will You Polish My Trophy?

Another reason we are too busy is that we have bought into the culture's definition of success. Postmodernism suggests that success is the ultimate goal in life. If you haven't fully attained it yet, then create the appearance or image of it. The world is your stage and everyone in it is your audience waiting to be impressed with your prowess. If you mean to break the cycle of busy-ness in your life, you must challenge this definition of success and ask yourself, "Is it worth the price?"

THE PRICE OF SUCCESS

Rick Fowler was in his office preparing for an upcoming appointment when the telephone rang. On the other end was an executive for a major U.S. corporation. "Rick," he began, "would you consider helping us by conducting some research on the issue of success and then sharing your results with our management team?"

When Rick asked what precipitated his call, he replied, "A good number of our upper-level executives don't get along.

They're only concerned with looking out for their own selfish ambitions. We've tried to figure out what's motivating this type of behavior and attitude. There seems to be a common thread: they all think their behavior is necessary for success. We need some help."

Rick readily accepted the project and devoted several months to researching several hundred articles and books. At first, the data seemed like just thousands of pieces in a giant jigsaw puzzle. Finally, as the pieces fell into place, a picture began to take shape in his mind. It was like a flagship leading a fleet of other ships. This flagship represents the business model of success-at-all-costs that is leading the way, not only for corporate executives, but also for many Christian leaders and church members.

The questions that seemed to shout at Rick as he read and studied were: "Is success really worth it? How can we get off this merry-go-round? Who can buck the system?"

The following mistaken assumptions represent a composite of the prevailing views of "successful" Americans and illustrate some of the rites of initiation to success.

Assumption #1: We must fit the profile.

The idea is that to be successful, we must become a clone of someone else who is successful. As children most of us emulated the "successful" model: the winning athlete, the movie star, or the rich businessman. This cloning is so real that when hundreds of junior-high students were asked if they would trade in their parents for more glamorous, successful people, two-thirds of the boys and three-fourths of the girls responded, "Yes!"

In the corporate setting, the success profile looks like this: having a college degree, dressing the part (many now have image consultants), allowing the company to be his conscience, working sixty hours a week, and being hooked on adrenalin to keep going. This person's psychological car is fueled by a drive to make it to the top, creating an imbalance in relationships and personal values.

Coming home on an airplane recently, Rick sat next to a man employed by a company that demanded twelve hours a day (minimum) from its management team. To enforce this expectation, it required employees to park their cars every morning in numbered spaces. The first one to arrive parked in space number one, the second one in space number two, and so on until all the spaces were filled. At the normal quitting time, the employee parked in space number two could not leave unless his associate in space number one had already left, and the game continued down the line of parking spaces. When Rick asked him why he didn't buck this unwritten law, he said, "I want to be successful with the company. By playing their game, I can get perks not available to those who don't give themselves totally to the company."

Assumption #2: Job takes priority over family.

The message is clear: to be successful, one must be wedded to work. This, coupled with the disproportionate number of hours spent on the job, has led to the corporation becoming the "other woman (or man)," serving as a catalyst for marital divorce (either actual physical detachment or an emotional parting of the ways within the marriage).

When Rick was reading his newspaper one morning, he noticed an interview with the president of a large fast-food chain. This man mentioned his New Year's resolution to spend more quality time with his family. Unfortunately, he explained, a corporate battle heated up with another fast-food chain and diverted him from his goal. Twelve- or thirteen-hour workdays became the norm, which meant giving up his family life. In the interview he expressed remorse over the imbalance, but held a fatalistic view of the situation. He was resigned to the necessity of sacrificing his family on the altar of success.

Research indicates that while many of America's successful young male executives talk of making family a priority, they don't really spend much time with their families or tie on an apron to help their wives. Their talk about quality time and shared parenting comes down to a trade-off. They may spend weekends with their families, but then they work until midnight every weeknight. Quality time on weekends often translates into putting the wife and kids into the car, then heading out to accomplish a mile-long list of errands. Some of the up-and-coming younger generation may even try to "buy off" family members by giving them money instead of time.

Assumption #3: Success equals stress.

After conducting extensive interviews and research, Rick concluded that the business world often defines success in terms of stress. Corporate loyalty is measured by the degree of stress one experiences. What is stress? It is anything that is perceived as a real or imagined threat. The rugged road that leads to success passes through many threats to the desired goal of getting to the top.

But if one is under ongoing daily pressure (the drive to produce not 100 percent but 110 percent), his productivity will decline by as much as 25 percent. That translates into an annual cost to American business of more than twenty billion dollars. It's easy to see the enormous price exacted by stress and stress-related illnesses.

Assumption #4: We are in a marathon race to survive.

American businessmen feel compelled to set goals ever higher with no letup to gain market share in a competitive global economy. Several of the authors' friends who have trained for grueling races talk about the sacrifice they made and the pain they endured to complete the run as though it were worth the effort. But physicians warn that prolonged unrelenting exercise like that can actually cause physical damage because there is no relief or rest during the long race. Similarly, in a corporation one who is intent on competing without any let-up can expect psychological damage and loss of productivity as the end result.

It is smarter in the long run to "leave something on the table" for the other guys after you have made a good profit for yourself. Aesop told a fable many centuries ago about a dog that dug up a little bone. Before he could eat it he encountered another dog who had a bigger bone. The dog dropped his little bone and fought the other dog for his bone and won. As he proudly went on his way with the bone in his mouth, he crossed a bridge over a stream. Glancing into an eddy of the stream, the dog thought he saw another dog with a bone. Thinking that he could take that bone away from the other dog, he growled and then barked at his reflection in the water. The bone in his mouth fell into the stream and disappeared.

Assumption #4: We need to be narcissistic.

The corporate model imagines that one must be totally selfish and use others to achieve success. You read the mythical story of Narcissus in Chapter 1. Narcissus was so callus in his relationships with other people, that a goddess cursed him with a spell that made him fall in love with his own reflection in a pool of water. Today, the term "narcissist" refers to someone who sees other people unrealistically as extensions of himself, as the means to meeting his own needs. In our dog-eat-dog society, stepping on another to get ahead has become the norm.

Those who hold to the narcissistic view of individualism, however, will ultimately find themselves in psychological conflict. Actually, in the past ten years, the American Psychiatric Association has labeled narcissism as a unique personality disorder. Isn't it ironic that the very ingredient deemed necessary for success in America causes psychological imbalance?

Assumption #5: We need to feel important and immortal.

There's a common attitude among those considered successful: "When I die, I will always be remembered; while I am alive, I will always be indispensable!" Take this quick quiz. Who were these men: Cyrus Holliday, William Littlewood, Paul Galvin? Though not household names, these men did make their mark on society in their time. Cyrus Holliday built a city, helped develop a state, and established a railroad: the Atchison, Topeka & Santa Fe. William Littlewood played a large role in developing the DC3 airplane. After a slow start in his career, Paul Galvin proved to be a brilliant man in the marketplace. He helped to build Motorola, Inc.

Face the facts: we are not immortal, and the world does not revolve around us. Yet these beliefs keep aspiring executives from delegating work to others, from enjoying the roses in the garden, and from seeing others on an equal plane with themselves.

TIME FOR REFLECTION

At one point in his kingly career, Solomon seems to have taken the wide and well-traveled road to success, and this is his conclusion: "'Meaningless! Meaningless!...Utterly meaningless!' What does a man gain from all his labor at which he toils under the sun?...I undertook great projects; I built houses for myself and planted vineyards...I amassed silver and gold for myself...I became greater by far than anyone in Jerusalem...Yet when I surveyed all that my hands had done and what I had toiled to achieve, everything was meaningless, a chasing after the wind; nothing was gained under the sun." (Ecclesiastes 1:2-3; 2:4, 8-11)

Perhaps a redefining of success is in order. Tom Osborne, head football coach at the University of Nebraska and a fine Christian, made some observations in his book, *More Than Winning*. In a moment of reflection in his hotel room following a national championship game in the Orange Bowl, coach Osborne said that winning the championship and the trophies is not the most important thing to him in athletics. Rather, it is the process. It is the experiences that you have, the relationships you form. He later added that he no longer uses wins and losses to measure success. Instead, he observes how close the team came to realizing its full potential. Finally, he concluded that success can be either good or bad, like money. It depends on how it affects you. The question is, "Do you use it, or does it use you?"

John Maxwell makes a similar statement in his book, *The Success Journey*. He asserts that success is not a goal you achieve and then enjoy the rest of your life. It is a journey that continues for your whole life. He defines success as understanding your purpose in life, developing toward your maximum potential, and doing things that benefit others.

If you look up the word "success" (KJV) or "successful" (NIV) in a concordance of the Bible, you might be surprised to find that there is only one verse in the entire Bible that uses the word in the sense we are using it. That fact in itself tells us something about the biblical perspective on this subject. The verse is Joshua 1:8, "Do not let this Book of the Law depart from your mouth; meditate on it day and night, so that you may be careful to do everything written in it. Then you will be prosperous and successful." This is a direct quote from God Himself when He assured Joshua that the key to his success would be his obedience to the Word of God. That is the crux of the matter. Will we let the culture define success for us, or will we look to God's Word for our definition?

What, then, is true success? Should it be viewed and defined through selfish lenses, where unrealistic conclusions about one's drives and worth are as empty as Solomon's handfuls of air? On the contrary, true success (1) is a process, (2) is based on inward satisfaction and not on external circumstances, (3) is reaching one's potential, (4) is serving others, and (5) is loving God and keeping His commandments—the conclusion Solomon eventually reached. "…Fear God and keep his commandments, for this is the whole duty of man. For God will bring every deed into judgment, including every hidden thing, whether it is good or evil." (Ecclesiastes 12:13-14)

Is the price for success worth it? Depending on your definition, your answer will either lead you to frustration and futility or to an inward peace and contentment.

JUMPING OFF THE MERRY-GO-ROUND

There is a way to break out of the cultural mold of busyness. The first step is to realize that things have not always been the way they are now and to consider a different approach to life. That was the main purpose for the historical review of Western culture in Chapter 1. While we cannot turn the clock back, and would not want to if we could, we can recapture some of the good, wholesome principles that we have lost along the way.

Most of them were contained or implied in the "Puritan work ethic." We do not have to abide by their asceticism. That was a distortion of Christianity the Reformation did not reach. The earliest and best Puritan leaders taught principles that were biblical and worth emulating.

Two ways God calls you

Foremost is the idea that one's work is a calling from God. Indeed, everything in the Christian's life is a response to God's calling. He called us first to salvation. This is the Christian's primary calling. In Romans 8:30, Paul wrote, "And those he predestined, he also called; those he called, he also justified; those he justified, he also glorified." This calling is to a relationship with Him through Christ. "God, who has called you into fellowship with his Son Jesus Christ our Lord, is faithful." (I Corinthians 1:9)

The primary calling also means that we relate everything in our lives to our relationship to God. When counseling the Corinthians about their attempts to change their circumstances after conversion, Paul advised them to remain in their present state as a part of their calling from God. For example, if they were married to an unbeliever, they should not seek a divorce. "Nevertheless, each one should retain the place in life that the Lord assigned to him and to which God has called him." (I Corinthians 7:17)

Particularly, our work is included in the call from God. This is our secondary calling. The primary calling is to a relationship with God, and the secondary calling is to service for God and man. These two aspects of calling must be equally respected and kept in proper relation to each other.

The early Puritans understood the importance of the relationship between the two callings, but before long the idea of calling became secularized. The terms *work, trade, employment* and *occupation* became synonymous with *calling* and *vocation*. This distortion substituted the secondary calling for the primary calling. The need for something to be accomplished became the source of the call, not God. Work was elevated to the status of the holy, deserving of worship. This view was called the "Protestant ethic." Eventually, the word *vocation* became divorced from the general term *work*, and applied to work involving lesser pay and sacrifice for others such as nursing, the pastorate and missionary service. It also was applied to non-professional skills such as carpentry and plumbing. Students who could not make the grade to enter liberal arts colleges were directed to "vocational" colleges. Today Evangelicals reveal their acceptance of this secularization of work when they refer to someone entering the pastorate or missions as doing "full-time Christian service." The underlying assumption is that all other Christians must be serving God "part-time," apparently in church activities. They see no connection between their occupations and service to God. We need to correct this distortion by returning to a biblical understanding of the two callings in proper relation to each other.

DISCOVER YOUR GOD-GIVEN PURPOSE

God has a purpose for every one He calls. "And we know that in all things God works for the good of those who love him, who have been called according to his purpose." (Romans 8:28) Paul understood that his work as a missionary was an assignment from God. He revealed His will for Paul in the church at Syrian Antioch. "While they were worshipping the Lord and fasting, the Holy Spirit said, 'Set apart for me Barnabas and Saul for the work to which I have called them.'" (Acts 13:2)

We need to remain flexible and open to the leadership of the Holy Spirit in our understanding of how God calls to specific work assignments. Just because God calls us to one kind of work at one point in our lives does not mean that we are being called to do the same thing for the rest of our lives. Paul's experience is a case in point. For years Paul worked as a traveling evangelist. Then he served as pastor of the church in Ephesus for three years. For about four years he was locked up in prison and was not able to perform any of the work that he was accustomed to doing. Yet it was during that time he wrote letters that eventually became part of the New Testament Scriptures.

One of the news stories commemorating Ronald Reagan reported that he was a firm believer in Divine Providence. He was convinced that God had a purpose for his life. If so, that purpose unfolded through several career changes. He began as a radio sports announcer. Then he became an actor, playing in over 50 B-grade movies. After landing supporting roles in several major films, he interrupted his acting career to serve in the military during World War II. After the war he resumed his acting profession and became successful as a major movie star. He could have retired and lived comfortably the rest of his life, but instead he chose to enter politics. His personal charm won him the governor's mansion in California, and eventually two terms in the White House.

The Bible records many instances when God called people to specific work assignments that were not directly related to spiritual leadership. Remember, the sacred and secular distinctions of the Middle Ages were based on pagan dualism, not the Bible. The first work assignment God gave to any man was in agriculture. "The Lord God took the man and put him in the Garden of Eden to work it and take care of it." (Genesis 2:15) God called Joshua to be a general in command of the Israeli army for the conquest of Canaan. (Deuteronomy 31:14; 23) He called Solomon to be a construction engineer and build the temple in Jerusalem. (I Chronicles 28:6; 10)

Of course, we should not expect a prophet of God or an angel messenger to deliver a formal commission to each of us personally. The above examples from Scripture occurred at major turning points in God's historic plan of salvation. Rather, we must rely on the Holy Spirit and prayer to give us the wisdom, skill, insight, faith and discernment we need to find out exactly what God has gifted each of us to do. Every wholesome talent, aptitude, inclination or interest we have is a gift from God. We should expect that He will providentially guide us to use them in life to serve others and glorify Himself. "Every good and perfect gift is from above, coming down from the Father of the heavenly lights, who does not change like shifting shadows." (James 1:17)

DEDICATE YOUR WORK TO GOD

Unfortunately, life in this fallen world does not always give people the freedom to select the way they make their living. Economic upheavals or necessity, bad decisions, prejudice, and any number of causes press people into work they would never freely choose. Another principle applies in that circumstance. Any legitimate task performed by a Christian living by faith can be dedicated to God and sanctified. Paul advised people who were oppressed in slavery to consider their service as performed for God. "Slaves, obey your earthly masters in everything; and do it, not only when their eye is on you and to win their favor, but with sincerity of heart and reverence for the Lord. Whatever you do, work at it with all your heart, as working for the Lord, not for men, since you know that you will receive an inheritance from the Lord as a reward. It is the Lord Christ you are serving." (Colossians 3:22-24) This inspiring principle applies equally as well to working under difficult supervisors or frustrating conditions in freely chosen occupations.

When you dedicate your work to God, you avoid the trap of worshipping your work. God alone deserves your worship. Anything that becomes a substitute for God in your life is an idol. A healthy view of work is to consider it a stewardship and a responsibility. It is a stewardship in the sense that you are entrusted with resources belonging to someone else (your employer) with the expectation that you will use them productively to contribute services equal to or greater than the value of your compensation (paycheck). If you own your own business, your investors have trusted you with capital expecting that you will use it to turn a profit. If you used your own capital, God has trusted you with it.

In any case, work is a responsibility to yourself, your family and the community. We are all consumers. Each of us is responsible to earn the resources to pay for what he consumes. The apostle, Paul, worked as a tent maker to finance his missionary journeys. He informed the Thessalonians that he worked instead of accepting their financial support to set an example for them to follow. "For even when we were with you, we gave you this rule: 'If a man will not work, he shall not eat.' We hear that some among you are idle. They are not busy; they are busybodies. Such people we command and urge in the Lord Jesus Christ to settle down and earn the bread they eat." (II Thessalonians 3:10-12) He made an even stronger statement about the head of the household's responsibility to provide for his family. "If anyone does not provide for his relatives, and especially for his immediate family, he has denied the faith and is worse than an unbeliever." (I Timothy 5:8)

God expects us to work, and to work hard; but there is a fine line between diligence and obsessive-compulsive behavior. If you view your work as a calling from God, then you will strive to keep it in balance with your other God-given responsibilities, such as giving nurture and spiritual leadership to your family, taking time to worship God and cultivate your relationship with Him, keeping yourself physically and emotionally healthy, and ministering to the needs of other Christians and members of your community. The difference is in your motivation. Compulsive workaholism is self-directed and self-centered. It is work carried to excess beyond stewardship and responsibility because you are getting something out of it, even if your family and your relationship to God suffer for it.

> *But godliness with contentment is great gain. For we brought nothing into the world, and we can take nothing out of it. But if we have food and clothing [shelter], we will be content with that. People who want to get rich fall into temptation and a trap and into many foolish and harmful desires that plunge men into ruin and destruction. For the love of money is a root of all kinds of evil. Some people, eager for money, have wandered from the faith and pierced themselves with many griefs. (I Timothy 6:6-10)*

To follow this admonition, we must go against the culture that sends us messages like, "You can have it all. Be a winner. Money is the way to keep score in the game of life. Live in the *now.* Create your own reality with positive thinking." These ideas come from a culture that has lost its Judaeo-Christian values. The culture views life as a mad dash to nowhere. "Get whatever you can out of life now, because there is no hope for anything beyond the grave," is the unspoken assumption.

The way out of this culturally inspired driven-ness is the way back to the values lost by our culture. It is the way out of addiction back to balance and wellness. The first step is to commit yourself to discovering God's will for your life and work.

When you dedicate your work to God, you are freeing yourself from much of the culturally inspired driven-ness. The decision to follow God's will for your life frees you from the notion of the autonomous self who tries to explore every conceivable option to find fulfillment and satisfaction in life. Instead you become free to concentrate on what you understand to be God's will for your life. The apostle, Paul, understood that God had called him to be conformed to the image of Christ (primary calling) and to be a missionary to the Gentiles (secondary calling). In his mind, the two callings came together in one sharp focal point for his life and work. "...But one thing I do: Forgetting what is behind and straining toward what is ahead, I press on toward the goal to win the prize for which God has called me heavenward in Christ Jesus." (Philippians 3:13b-14)

BUCKING THE SYSTEM

Earlier in this chapter, Rick asked the question, "Who can buck the system?" When Gerald Ford ran for President, he campaigned on the issue of fighting inflation. His slogan was, "If not you, who? If not now, when?" Those are good questions to ask yourself.

If you are the CEO in your company, you have the authority to change policies and set standards. Make the decision to do it. Of course, you will need the backing of your board of directors and the cooperation of your executives in the chain of command. Perhaps the best approach would be to tell them you have a plan for increasing productivity and improving employee morale and retention. Talk to them about stress management, human resource development, more efficient scheduling and improved customer service, not our calling from God. That concept would be more than they could accept unless your company is a Christian organization.

Your next task would be to hammer out your new policies, standards and procedures. You will have to figure out the specifics for your company and profession, but here are some trigger thoughts. When planning your calendar, schedule some time between the completion of one big project and the beginning of a new one to give your employees time to recover from the stress. Think of ways to recognize and reward employees for good teamwork, such as sharing helpful information with associates, volunteering to accept part of another employee's work load if he is overloaded, being an encourager. Clearly communicate to your employees in their evaluations that you value diligence and efficiency during normal working hours more than working late. Formulate and disseminate policies that stress the importance of stable families to the company, that call for delegation, deferment or reassignment of tasks and responsibilities if they unreasonably interfere with normal family time and function. Hire an efficiency-consulting firm to make recommendations on how your employees can achieve the same or better results than they are getting now in less time. Use the saved hours to relieve over-scheduling and excessive stress levels. Hopefully you are getting the idea now.

If you are a mid-level executive, you could try a similar approach. The difference is that you would have to sell the idea to your supervisor instead of a board of directors. Also, you might find some other like-minded executives in your church and meet with them for brainstorming sessions, networking and encouragement.

If you are not in management, your task will be more difficult but do-able. Use the same strategy to appeal to your supervisor. The difference is that you will be talking about your own personal performance. Make your case on the basis of stress management, reducing the number of sick days off, and increasing your efficiency. The "bee will be on your back." You must demonstrate by your job performance that you are more productive without excessive stress, and with adequate time off for rest and time with your family. Be particularly scrupulous about arriving on time and putting in a good day's work for a day's pay. Be prayerful and creative in finding and implementing solutions to problems in your department. Stay positive and upbeat. In short, become such a valuable employee that your supervisor will be willing to "cut you some slack," and relieve you from excessive demands on your time.

The harsh reality is that some companies will respond to this approach and many will not. If you have tried everything you know to do to get relief, but without results, then you probably will have to make a hard decision. Look for a better job, unless you feel there is a compelling, God-honoring reason to stay where you are. Fear is not a good reason. When the economy is going soft, the thought of changing jobs is intimidating; but don't let fear stop you. It is generally easier to find a good job when you are already gainfully employed. Don't hang on until you get laid off, your health breaks, or you lose your family. Remember, God is your ultimate resource and provider, not your job. It's not for everyone, but many executives and other employees have resolved this dilemma by starting their own home-based business. If you can manage a business or produce a valuable product for someone else, why not do it for yourself? Pray about it.

DOES YOUR JOB FIT YOU?

There is no perfect job. Yet, there may be some things about your job that bother you. Is it the rushed pace, constant pressure, crisis atmosphere, or too little time off? Are these reasons to look for another job, or just annoyances to be tolerated?

This quiz will help you answer that question. Study the list of job characteristics in the chart that follows. Select the 15 qualities that are most desirable to you and check them off in the left column. Then go down the right column and check off the ones that your present job includes. Finally, count the number of matches to determine your score.

IS YOUR JOB RIGHT FOR YOU?

WHAT YOU WANT	JOB CHARACTERISTICS	WHAT YOU HAVE
	Involves creative thinking	
	Offers job security	
	Allows for quick career advancement	
	Teaches you new skills	
	Lets you handle your own projects	
	Offers an easy commute	
	Has a fast pace	
	Has a relaxed, pressure-free pace	
	Has liberal benefits	
	Involves travel	
	Allows personal growth and pride	
	Lets you work with your hands	
	Has flexible hours	
	Promotes from within	
	Pays on a commission basis	
	Permits casual dress	
	Involves teaching others	
	Allows privacy to talk on phone	
	Lets you use sales skills	
	Pays on a par with competitive companies	
	Involves constant communication with others	
	Recognizes individual achievement with bonuses	
	Lets you draw upon your education	
	Lets you help others improve their lives	
	Offers opportunity to meet people	
	Requires supervising others	
	Has a professional, highly structured atmosphere	
	Has a friendly atmosphere	
	Encourages employees to take on more responsibility	

SCORING

15- Keep the job! It fits you well. You are using your strengths to good advantage in a positive work environment. • **10-** Your job is not a perfect match, but it is good enough for you to achieve satisfaction. Stay put. • **5-** Your job does not fit you. Think about the kind of work you would rather do and the office environment that would suit you better. Polish up your resume.

CHAPTER 5

God, Do You Have Next Tuesday at 9:00 P.M. Open for Me?

It is a beautiful spring morning, and the farmer is up with the sun. Today he is going to plow one of his fields for planting. He walks 200 yards to the edge of the field where his tractor sits. Before cranking it, he remembers to check the oil level in the crankcase. Sure enough, it is low. No problem, there is a can of oil back in the shed.

As he approaches the barnyard, he notices a stack of green logs that he cut down this past winter. "Summer is almost here. I need to split these logs so they can dry out in the heat." So, he spends some time splitting the logs.

Noticing that the sun is high in the sky, he remembers the oil for the tractor, so he puts down his axe and heads for the shed. But a sickly-looking chicken ambles across his path. "If I don't give that chicken some medicine, I'm going to lose her," he thinks. So, he turns aside to the barn to get the medicine.

In the barn he notices a pungent odor. "How long has it been since I cleaned out the cows' stalls? This is disgusting. I've put this job off too long." So, he starts cleaning out the stalls and bringing in fresh hay for his cows.

When he finishes, he finds the medicine and starts looking for the sick chicken. But the chicken has wandered away. When he finally locates her, she runs away from him, so he has to chase her around the barnyard. Eventually he catches her and gives her the medicine.

At last, he goes to the shed and gets the oil for the tractor. As he starts to walk the 200 yards back to the field, he realizes to his dismay that the sun is setting.

• • • •

ACHIEVING EFFECTIVENESS

Time is a great equalizer. Everyone has the same amount of it every day. Whether you are effective and productive or not depends on how you spend it. The farmer in the story was very busy all day long, but he was not effective.

To maximize your time, begin each day with prayer, asking God to guide you in the use of your time. Then spend the first thirty minutes of work time planning how you will spend your day. Planning brings the future into the present so that you can do something about it now. Failure to cultivate this simple habit could be a major reason why you are too busy and don't seem to have enough time. Good planning helps you achieve effectiveness—doing the right things at the right time.

SETTING GOALS

The first step in time management is goal setting. You need to go through the process for yourself personally, your family, and your job. Write them down. If you never take time to write down your goals, you are probably not serious about attaining them. Start with primary goals. For example, a good personal goal is "to know God." Then write secondary goals to go with them. Good secondary goals for "to know God" would be "to be a diligent student of the Bible," "to be a person who lives with an awareness of God," "to be a faithful member of a local church where the Bible is proclaimed and studied."

ACTIVITIES

But goals cannot be scheduled, so you must break them down into activities. Continuing our example, activities for "to be a diligent student of the Bible" could be:

1. Read a chapter a day from the Bible.
2. Complete a series of personal Bible study courses.
3. Attend a small group Bible study.

Using your goals as a guide, make a "To Do" list for each day. Be sure to incorporate activities that will accomplish your goals as well as urgent things that just need to be done.

At this point, you should give some thought to delegating. Do not accept a task for yourself that someone else in your organization can do "well enough." Remember, perfection is usually not necessary, and is hardly ever affordable.

PRIORITIZING

The next step is to prioritize. Tag each item in your list with "A," "B," and "C" priorities. "A" is for tasks that are either urgent or important, the ones that truly must be done. The tried and proven 80/20 Rule states that in a list of ten tasks, two of them, when accomplished, will yield 80 percent of the value of the entire list. They are your highest priority "A" tasks. "B" is for things that are less urgent but are important, such as preparing a report that has a deadline three weeks out, answering e-mail and phone calls, sorting other mail, or getting some exercise. By the way, when sorting and dealing with mail, try to handle each item only once. Either answer it immediately, file it, give it to someone else for action, or throw it away. "C" is for good things you would like to do that are optional, such as reading trade journals.

Then prioritize items under each category with 1, 2, or 3. It is best to start with your most difficult or unpleasant tasks first, so number them as 1's. Tackle your "A-1" priorities early in the day when you are at your best, then move on to "A-2's" and "A-3's." Work on your "C" items during odd moments such as a 15-minute break between meetings or appointments. Finish the day working on your "B" items.

When NASA sent a man to the moon, the space scientists had a trajectory figured out in advance. However, it was necessary to make course corrections during the flight to make sure that the rocket remained on the correct path to the moon. Likewise, a good manager needs to make corrections occasionally in his priorities. Some managers claim that they increase their efficiency by as much as 50% by taking three to five minutes every hour or so to rearrange their priorities when the situation calls for it. Ask, "What is the best use of my time *right now?*"

SCHEDULING

Next, schedule. Appointments and social activities will have specified times. For the rest of your activities, it is best to divide the day into three segments: Morning, Afternoon and Evening, then simply list the ones you plan to do in each segment without assigning specific time periods. It is imperative that you reserve time for your personal devotions and solitude, family, friends, church and ministry activities. Write them into your planning sheets. If you don't, other activities will surely take their place. When you are asked to commit to conflicting activities you can honestly say, "I have already made other plans for that time."

Finally, look at your schedule and ask yourself, "Does this time management plan make sense to me? Is it too crowded? Does it leave time for pursuit of a hobby, or just 'down time' when I don't plan to do anything in particular?" It has been said, "If you are not comfortable spending time doing nothing in particular, then you do not believe in the sovereignty of God." You shouldn't expect to be productive all of the time. God is God and you are not. Let Him run the universe without you sometimes.

TAKING THE WIND OUT OF LONG-WINDED PHONE CALLS

One of the specific time-wasters that will inevitably occur and threaten to wreck your carefully made time management plan is the long-winded phone call. Management consultant R. James Steffen recommends that you ask yourself, "Is this call related to one of my A-1 priorities?" For example, if the caller is one of your major clients, then the answer would be, "Yes."

Otherwise, you need a strategy to end the phone conversation politely but quickly. One effective method is to summarize what the caller has said and then ask, "Do you have any more important things to tell me?" Most of the time, he will say, "No." Then you say something like, "It was good to hear from you, Jim, thank you for calling. Good-bye." [1]

INTERRUPTING INTERRUPTIONS

There are two kinds of interruptions: the ones you cause yourself and the ones other people cause. Although you are probably most annoyed by the interruptions imposed on you from outside, research shows that most of the time wasted by interruptions is the result of interruptions you cause yourself.[2] For example, if you are frustrated or bored with the task you are working on, don't give in to the temptation to relieve the stress by making a phone call or walking down the hall to someone else's office. It would be better to stay in your office and do some stretching or relaxation exercises for just a few minutes and then go back to work.

Interruptions caused by other people come in two varieties: the ones you can control and the ones you can't. Consider first the ones you can control. Some managers pride themselves on having an "open door policy," signaling that they are available to anyone any time. That policy allows everyone else to determine the priorities on how you spend your time. It is not effective.

A better approach is the "enlightened open door policy." First, you decide when is the best time for you to see other people. Then, contact the people who regularly need to see you and find out when they most often need to see you. With their agreement, set a time that you will regularly be available to them. Establish that outside of that time, you will only be available on an emergency basis.

By definition, there is not much you can do about interruptions beyond your control. However, you can minimize the frustration and stress they cause by adopting a positive attitude about them. When an unavoidable interruption comes along, regard it as an A-1 priority and give it your best effort.[2] Sometimes these are "Divine interruptions."

MONKEYS ON YOUR BACK

If you are a manager, much of your excessive busy-ness could result from the way you allow subordinates to relate to you. In "Management Time: Who's Got the Monkey?" William Oncken, Jr. and Donald L. Wass explain why managers usually run out of time while their subordinates usually run out of work. In their analogy a monkey is a problem that needs solving.[3] The following is a summary of their article.

A manager spends time in three areas of responsibility. The first is *supervisor-imposed time*. It is time spent doing whatever the person in authority over him requires. There is little room for discretion. Failure to perform results in direct and speedy unpleasantness. The second area is *system-imposed time*. It is time spent responding to requests from his peers for active involvement and cooperation in their work. There are consequences for failure to perform in this area, but they are not always direct or speedy. The third area is *self-imposed time*. It is time spent doing things the manager thinks of doing on his own initiative or agrees willingly to do. Part of this time will be consumed by subordinates, and is called *subordinate-imposed time*. The rest of his self-imposed time is free to use as he sees fit, and is called *discretionary time*. There are no penalties in this area, since neither his supervisor nor his peers in the system know what he intends to do.

Time management requires the manager to control the timing and nature of his activities. Since there are penalties attached to the supervisor- and system-imposed responsibilities, the area over which he has most control and flexibility is the self-imposed time. His game plan should be to increase the "discretionary" part of his self-imposed time by reducing or eliminating the "subordinate" part. Then he can use the time gained to deal more effectively with his supervisor- and system-imposed responsibilities and still have some time left for his own initiatives.

JUMPING MONKEYS

Monkeys have a way of jumping from one person's back to another. Suppose a manager walks down a hallway and meets subordinate, Joe, coming from the other direction. Joe says, "Good morning, how are you?" When the manager reciprocates, Joe says, "I'm fine, except for this problem I am dealing with. Do you have a minute?" Two things are fairly certain in this situation. (1) The manager knows enough about the problem to get involved. (2) He does not know enough to make an on-the-spot decision. Almost inevitably he will say something like, "I'll think about it and get back to you." Before this meeting in the hall, the monkey was on Joe's back; but where is he now? He just jumped onto the manager's back. Now the manager is on subordinate-imposed time. Joe has given him a job to do. The next day, Joe stops by the manager's office and breezily asks, "How is it coming?" (Joe's behavior is known as "supervision.")

WHO IS WORKING FOR WHOM?

If the manager has four subordinates working under him, and each of them allows no more than three monkeys to jump from his back to the manager's each day, at the end of a five-day work week the manager has sixty shrieking monkeys hanging onto him. If he tries to deal with each one individually, he will never finish if he keeps up with his supervisor- and system-imposed responsibilities. The result is that the manager spends his subordinate-imposed time "juggling priorities" and falling farther behind. In the meantime, he has created a bottleneck, because his subordinates are all waiting for him to make a decision before they can finish their assignments.

The last straw for the manager in our imagined situation was an incident that occurred one Saturday morning. He had come back to the office to try to "catch up" on the sixty problems and decisions his subordinates had given him that week. His office happened to be located next to a golf course. When the manager looked out of the window, whom did he see playing a foursome? Yes, it was his subordinates!

GETTING RID OF THE MONKEYS

The manager discovered a way to end this "monkey-business." After his moment of insight, he invited each of his subordinates to meet him in his office on Monday morning. The objective of each interview was to set the monkey on the desk before them and decide together what action the subordinate could take to deal with the problem. If that was not readily apparent, then the manager would assign the subordinate the responsibility of coming up with an idea overnight and reporting for another meeting the next morning. The monkey would have to spend the night on the subordinate's back, but that did not matter. A monkey sleeps just as well on a subordinate's back as he does on a manager's.

As each subordinate left the manager's office after one of these meetings, the manager had the satisfaction of seeing one or more monkeys leave on the back of the subordinate. No longer were the subordinates waiting for the manager to make a decision or a move. The manager was waiting for them.

How gratifying it was for the manager a day or two later when he stuck his head into the office of one of his subordinates and asked brightly, "How's it coming?" The time the manager spent in this exercise was discretionary, but the subordinate's time was supervisor-imposed.

In the next meeting, the manager spelled out some ground rules: (1) "For as long as I am helping you with a problem, it will never become my problem. If your problem becomes my problem, then you don't have a problem, and there is no need to help you if you don't have a problem." (2) "When you leave my office, the problem will go with you. You may make an appointment to ask for my help, and we will make a joint decision as to what the next move should be and who should make it."

Passing on Initiative

The "object of the exercise" is to pass on the initiative for problem solving from the manager to his subordinates. To free up his subordinate-imposed time, the manager must make sure that his subordinates keep the initiative. The manager and a subordinate cannot have the same initiative on the same problem at the same time. Never let a subordinate assume, "We've got a problem." It is *his* problem and the initiative to solve it belongs to him alone.

There are five degrees of initiative:

1. *Wait* until your supervisor tells you what to do.

2. *Ask* your supervisor what to do.

3. *Recommend* to your supervisor what needs to be done and then take the appropriate action with his approval.

4. *Act* first and then tell your supervisor immediately what you have done.

5. *Act on your own*, and then routinely report to your supervisor.

A good manager will not utilize degrees one or two. Waiting gives the manager no control over the time or the content of his tasks. Asking gives him control over the timing of his tasks, but not the content. Also, it is his responsibility to discourage his subordinates from using degrees one or two. The manager should make sure that he and his subordinate agree on a level of initiative for each problem and schedule another meeting to confer about it before he sends the subordinate away with it.

Rules of Monkey Care and Feeding

When the manager helps his subordinates care for their monkeys, there are five rules that must be strictly followed:

Rule 1

Either feed your monkeys or shoot them. If you don't, they will starve to death, and the manager will waste time trying to determine the cause of death or perform a resuscitation.

Rule 2

Limit the monkey population to a number the manager can feed in the time he allows for it.

Rule 3

Feed monkeys only by appointment. The manager should never be required to hunt down starving monkeys on a catch-as-catch-can basis for feeding.

Rule 4

Only feed monkeys in face-to-face interviews or by telephone. Using mail—including memos and e-mail—leaves the next move up to the manager. The interviews should not last much over fifteen minutes.

Rule 5

Assign an appointed time for the next feeding to every monkey along with a degree of initiative.

CONTROLLING TIME AND CONTENT

The key to effective management is establishing and maintaining control of the timing and content of your tasks. By transferring initiative to your subordinates, you will decrease or eliminate most of your subordinate-imposed time responsibilities. That will free up more discretionary time to gain control of the timing and content of your supervisor- and system-imposed responsibilities, and to implement the discretionary tasks that are important to you.

TIME MANAGEMENT SELF ANALYSIS

Listed below is a series of statements about various ways of approaching a job. Answer these items in terms of your characteristic habit patterns. No one except you will see the results. Be honest. See how you rate in "the management of time" compared to others.

	Almost Never	Some-times	Often	Almost Always
1. I keep a written log of how I spend the major portions of my working day.				
2. I schedule my least interesting tasks at a time when my energy is at a peak.				
3. I review my job and delegate activities that someone else could do just as well.				
4. I have time to do what I want to do and what I should do in performing my job.				
5. I analyze my job to determine how I can combine or eliminate activities.				
6. Actions that lead to short-run objectives take preference over those that might be more important over the long pull.				
7. My boss assigns more work than he thinks I can handle.				
8. I attack short-time tasks (answering phone calls, reading correspondence, etc.) before projects taking a long time.				
9. I review the sequence of my job activities and make necessary improvements.				
10. I arrange task priorities based on the importance of task goals.				

EXPLANATION OF "BEST" TIME UTILIZATION

Item 1. The suggested best answer to keeping a written log of activities is "sometimes." The successful manager will recognize that this activity has merit when it comes to eliminating redundant or useless effort, but he should realize that he might not need to record every day. Besides, a time consciousness developed through formal analysis will encourage an informal continuing review.

It is entirely possible to become preoccupied with accounting for how each minute is spent and lose sight of the original purpose of time analysis: to become a more efficient manager. One could be in the position of spending more time looking for wasted time than he can justify.

Item 2. The suggested best answer to scheduling least interesting tasks when energy is highest is "almost always." Professor Leo Danielson suggests that managers spend most of their time on activities which interest them, followed by those which they do well, which are pleasurable, and which are forced upon them, and tend to put off until last those activities which are least interesting. The more pleasurable tasks should be handled at the end of the day when energy is at lowest ebb. The effective manager will attack those uninteresting (and probably more difficult) tasks when his personal energies are at their peak during his working day. Self-imposed deadlines can help him accomplish this objective.

Item 3. The suggested best answer for delegating activities is "almost always." The logic in this reasoning is found in the words, "someone else could do it just as well." The effective manager is not normally concerned with doing a job perfectly. Rather, he is interested in an optimal quality level that is arrived at by trading off quality with cost. He is interested in doing the job "well enough."

Many "professionals-turned-managers" are victimized in this regard by their own inquisitive minds. They tend to feel they must do the highest quality work possible; that tolerances must be extremely close, even though this is not required and is very expensive to attain. This has been termed the "Rolls Royce

Syndrome." Most professionals-turned-managers do not drive Rolls Royces even if they can afford them, because they are "too good." The cost of obtaining such quality is too great. In the same vein, the manager who insists on doing all the work himself, because he is the only one who can do it to perfection, is wasting his time and needlessly increasing the cost to his organization.

Item 4. "Almost always" is the suggested best answer to having sufficient time to do what is needed. If the manager is complying with the principles in Items 2 and 3, the time should be available as needed.

Item 5. The suggested best answer is "sometimes" to managerial job analysis and combining of activities. As in the answer to Item 1, a real time consciousness will dictate that this activity be performed occasionally, but it is not necessary for formal analysis on a constant basis.

Item 6. The suggested best answer regarding the relative preference of short-run objectives over long-run goals is "sometimes." It must be recognized that although many people feel the long haul is the important objective, and more immediate objectives should be subjected to the long run, this is not always true. The most desirable situation is the attainment of short-run objectives concomitant with long-run objectives. Economist John Maynard Keynes said, "In the long run we'll all be dead." It's important to realize that while long-run goals must be served (sometimes at the expense of short-run objectives), if the short-run is not attended to, the long-run objective will never be attained.

Item 7. The suggested best answer to the assigning of an excessive workload by the boss is "almost never." The assumption of such behavior on the part of the superior is to assume personality quirks of some sort. However, given a normal superior and a higher frequency alternative as a response to this question, it may be an indication that the manager's boss believes he's wasting time doing unnecessary tasks.

Item 8. "Almost never" is also the suggested best answer to attacking short-time duration tasks before long-time duration projects. As Moore found, the ten most common time problems are essentially of a short-time nature. It is entirely possible for the manager to spend his entire day handling little details, while trying to lay out blocks of time to do the big jobs. The catch is that the little jobs are recurring. The phone will always ring; the mail will always come in. These things simply do not go away unless made to go away, and blocks of time are essential for completing large projects.

The principle behind successfully handling this problem is that little jobs tend to evaporate if unattended. Unread advertisements and unrewarded interruptions by subordinates tend to vanish without a trace if left alone. However, when confronted, they take time and have the debilitative effect of encouraging subordinates, correspondents, etc., to engage in future interruptions. There are obviously limits to how far a manager can go in ignoring these interruptions, but the limit is much farther out than most realize.

The manager should "wade right in" on the big jobs at the start of his day and try to pursue them to completion. At least the job will have been started, setting up the psychological aversion to unfinished work present in most humans (the so-called Zeigarnik Effect). The manager is more likely to return to the unfinished job after an unavoidable interruption than to start a completely new task.

Item 9. In reviewing the sequence of job activities, the proposed best answer is "often." The proper sequencing of job activities is all-important to the success of long-run goals. Without frequent review of this nature, the timing of long-run projects may be affected.

Item 10. The suggested best answer to arranging task priorities based on task goals is "almost always." If one doesn't know where he is going, almost any path will take him there. A manager might be inclined to pursue those tasks that are of less than top priority unless he knows the goals of those that are not the most important. (See "Time Contract" on next page.)

TIME CONTRACT

I agree to conserve my time and use it better by doing the following:

1. Set clear goals for my personal life and my job.
2. Put my goals in order of priority and work regularly on high priority items.
3. Develop a list of daily priority items to do each day.
4. Stick to my time management plan except for emergencies.
5. Control the number and length of my phone calls.
6. Set up an "enlightened open door" policy for my office.
7. Stop wasting my time on non-essential matters and putting off the most important things.
8. Delegate to others all things they can, could or should do.
9. Develop a file system to keep track of all work items.
10. Set deadlines for tasks and projects and have someone remind me of them.
11. Plan a daily "quiet time" for thinking and planning.
12. Say, "No, I would like to do this but I don't have time," to attractive invitations or offers that are not a part of my goals or priorities.
13. Set time limits for meetings, interviews, and conferences and enforce them.
14. Periodically stop and assess the use of my time. Ask myself regularly, "Is what I'm doing the best use of my time?"
15. Before each day is over, spend some time in solitude, silence and prayer, meditating on God and His Word.

Signed,

_____

CHAPTER 6

Busy-ness to Dizziness

WHAT IS THE MATTER WITH ME?

"I feel tired most of the time. I'm doing what I usually do, but the joy and enthusiasm are gone...If anyone crosses me, I lose it...I feel overwhelmed by tasks I used to take in stride...I'm just not the man (woman) I used to be...I can't think about anyone else's problems; dealing with my own is all I can manage...I have trouble keeping things straight in my mind...Life is all a crock anyway..." If you are saying things like this to yourself, then you are probably experiencing stress overload from being too busy.

Stress is not just being nervous or emotional; it is your body's nonspecific response to demands made on it. By nonspecific, we mean that the body reacts in basically the same way to many different conditions. For example, if a major client you have been negotiating with for months informs you that they are signing a contract with your competitor, your feeling of shock, sense of loss and grief, and fear for job security would likely cause your body to respond with increased heartbeat, rapid breathing, increased blood pressure, and a slowing down of the digestive process. On the other hand, if you find out later that your competitor defaulted on the contract and the client is awarding it to your company after all, your feeling of surprise, relief and elation, and anticipation of the challenges to fulfill the contract would probably cause the same set of responses in your body that the loss of the contract caused.

Why does your body respond the same way to nearly opposite circumstances? God designed your body to protect itself from outside aggressors that threaten it. The nonspecific responses to stress prepare the body either to resist an aggressor (fight) or to evade the threatening situation (flight). By adjusting to the ever-changing circumstances around it, your body enables you to navigate through life and attempt to achieve whatever goals you have set for yourself. This process is called the *general adaptation syndrome,* or G.A.S. for short. It goes through three stages: (1) alarm, (2) resistance, and (3) exhaustion. The purpose of this process is to keep the body in a more or less steady state, close to equilibrium. The stress response is designed to offset the stressful circumstance and return the body to its normal state of balance.

Since some amount of stress is an integral part of normal life functions, the only time the body is completely free from stress is when it is dead. Even when you are asleep, your body is responding to dream sequences and damage caused by the day's activities and experiences. Stress, then, cannot be avoided; it must be properly managed.

Much of the stress you experience is good for you. Moderate, appropriate exercise, either as recreation or as part of your daily work responsibility, helps to keep your arteries open and free-flowing, and promotes good muscle tone. The excitement you feel when giving a speech before a large group of people sharpens your mental faculties. As long as the stress reaction is temporary and the body has the opportunity to return to the steady state (homeostasis), no harm is done.

Problems arise when stressful situations occur too often during the same day and the body rarely returns to homeostasis. Your body needs to operate in cycles, alternating between periods of high stress and low stress, periods of activity followed by time for rest and recuperation. Excessive busy-ness disrupts these normal cycles and rhythms.

WHAT MAKES ME FEEL STRESSED?

Some stress comes from external conditions that affect your body. A few examples would be: hot or cold temperatures, a noisy or contentious work place, or abusive family relationships. Other stress comes from internal conditions, such as inflammation or infection in the body; or psychological disturbances like anxiety, feelings of resentment or aggression.

Time is also an important factor in stress. Short-term (acute) stress is the body's reaction to an immediate threat: the fight or flight response. This is the most common form of stress that includes situations such as: noise, overcrowding, isolation from social contact, food deprivation, risky or dangerous circumstances, bodily infections, and remembering or imagining traumatic experiences. Normally, your body's reaction subsides when the threat is over and stress hormones settle down to normal again (the relaxation response).

Long-term (chronic) stress is more harmful. The stressful circumstances continue from day to day. The normal urge to react by fighting or running away must be resisted and suppressed. A few situations that result in chronic stress are: a high-pressure job environment, conflicts in family relationships, loneliness, financial pressure, and an over programmed schedule.

WHAT IS STRESS DOING TO ME?

Imagine how your body would respond if a bear were chasing you. In your brain, the *hypothalamic-pituitary-adrenal* (HPA) system would go into action, producing and releasing steroid hormones (glucocorticoids), one of which is *cortisol*. Cortisol prepares your heart, lungs, circulatory system, metabolism, immune system, and skin to fight threats to the body. Your breathing would speed up so the lungs could take in more oxygen. Your heart would beat faster, increasing blood flow by 300% to 400% to sustain your muscles, lungs and brain in their increased activity. White blood cells and other parts of the immune system would be redistributed and concentrated in areas most likely to be injured, such as the skin, bone marrow and lymph nodes. Body fluids would be diverted from non-essential areas such as the mouth, causing it to be dry and making swallowing difficult. Blood also would be diverted from the skin to the heart and muscles, leaving the skin cold and clammy. Another non-essential bodily activity for the duration of an emergency, the digestive system, would shut down.

Also, the HPA system would release *catecholamines*, neurotransmitters or chemical messengers such as *dopamine, norepinephrine, and epinephrine* (adrenaline). Together, they trigger an emotional response to the stressful event and store it in long-term memory. Apparently this helps you to avoid the threatening situation in the future. (Don't feed the bears.) At the same time, the *catecholamines* suppress short-term memory, concentration, inhibition and rational thinking. This allows for a quick response, either to fight the bear or run away from it.

All of these responses serve you well in emergency situations. Serious problems result when the stress response becomes a part of your daily routine. Just a few of them include: increased risk of heart attack, digestive disorders, chronic fatigue, arthritis and other inflammatory diseases, and a weakened immune system that leaves you vulnerable to chronic and possibly serious infections. In short, chronic stress makes you less effective. To achieve balance and wellness, and fulfill your God-given purpose in life, it is necessary to manage the stress you are experiencing.

TAMING THE STRESS MONSTER

Dr. Fowler recently conducted a seminar on stress for a women's organization. Arriving early, he overheard several of the participants talking. As he listened he reached a few conclusions: (1) The popular interest in stress results from the implication that a stressed person has status and important responsibilities to fulfill. The logic here may be paraphrased as "busy-ness to the point of dizziness" correlates to importance.

(2) Stress is often treated as a toy rather than a problem to be solved. (3) Stress is a culturally acceptable cliché to have in one's pocket; it becomes the scapegoat. In other words, the suggestion that one is a victim of this "monster" seems to excuse the individual from responsibility in difficult circumstances.

These factors offer some possible explanations for the multiplication of stress-related materials. Before the mid-70s, psychology textbooks rarely mentioned stress as a problem. Now nearly all of them handle it in several chapters. What has changed? Some of the words that describe our current culture may offer a clue: "fast-food," "express lanes," "up-tight," and "instant access." This type of society has produced a generation hooked on adrenalin. When rushing through life at high speed it is easy to lose direction. Part of the explanation for the demand for so many self-help books on stress management may be that people are searching for guidebooks that can remind them what life is all about.

Another reason for the increase in interest in stress management is the "Narcissistic personality" Christopher Lasch described in *The Culture of Narcissism*. The Narcissist has an exaggerated and unrealistic love of self, which results in a preoccupation with the self and a tendency to embrace information that draws thoughts and energy inward. Instead of a healthy ability to rise above the stress, the Narcissist dwells on how it is affecting him and what he looks like while suffering from it. Stress becomes a tool to disseminate his self-propaganda.

Can an over-awareness of this issue increase its negative power over the individual? Our society has conditioned people to dwell on stress as a problem rather than to seek a solution to it. This can have a paralyzing effect on people and push them to feel helpless and victimized instead of actively conquering the stressful aspects of life.

Unfortunately, many Christians have fallen prey to the same preoccupation with this issue as the world. Why is it that the average Christian seems to find himself as vulnerable to the effects of negative stress as the rest of society? Has the church assimilated a worldly message? Hebrews 12:1, 2 directs Christians to

"...throw off everything that hinders," and "...run with perseverance the race marked out for us. Let us fix our eyes on Jesus." This does not leave room for fearful speculations about the power of stress. The believer's life is full of meaning and purpose. With one's eyes fixed on Jesus, the world's message that people should never feel pain becomes obviously false.

No other human has suffered as much as our savior, but He never focused on the stress in His life. He never questioned the Father's wisdom in allowing Him to experience pain for our sake. This fact is even more poignant when we consider that He never sinned, so all the stress He encountered was in no way due to mistakes.

The Bible describes the Christian as a soldier. We are told to put on the breastplate of faith and a helmet, which is the hope of salvation. This is not the image of a victim! This is a confident warrior who knows where his future lies. In I Thessalonians 5:4-11, Paul reminds us that it is the unsaved who get drunk at night, but the Christian is of the day and is sober. The striking distinction between the world and the believer should caution us against patterning our thinking and lifestyle after unbelievers. We know the truth, and our sobriety can protect us from the despair of the culture.

GETTING RID OF FEAR-THOUGHT

Once we have realigned our worldview with the truth of scripture, we are prepared to deal with the difficult habit of worry that grows out of our stress and busy-ness. Remember that worry is fundamentally based on fear; and fear has no place in the Christian's life. Jesus said, "Are not two sparrows sold for a penny? Yet not one of them will fall to the ground apart from the will of your Father. And even the very hairs of your head are all numbered. So don't be afraid; you are worth more than many sparrows." (Matthew 10:29-30)

However, emotions often fail to line up with what we know in our heads. The primary goal is always to align our behavior with truth, so much of what this chapter recommends is to remind us of what is true. In a postmodern culture that doubts truth's existence, this can be quite a challenge, but it is well worth the effort. The authors suggest some ways the Christian can resist temptation to worry.

Try to see the broad perspective of the situation, yet work through the problem in small manageable chunks.

There is an old story about three construction workers. As they labored side by side on the same project, a passer-by stopped to observe their work. "What are you doing?" he asked the first worker. "Laying bricks," he replied. Then the observer asked the second worker the same question. " Putting up a wall," he answered. Finally the man asked the third worker what he was doing, to which he exclaimed, "I am constructing a magnificent cathedral!"

Only the third worker had a broad perspective of the situation, and that gave him inspiration and hope. But, building a cathedral is a daunting task that could seem overwhelming. The other workers may have reduced their stress levels by focusing on the simple tasks and intermediate steps involved in the project. Both approaches are helpful.

Building a successful business or professional practice, reaching a sales quota, or putting together a joint venture are highly motivating undertakings, but they can create many problems to worry about and generate excessive stress. When stress begins to mount, choose a specific task that will contribute to your long-range goal and focus on that task. It might be to collect price information from prospective vendors, or draw up a flow chart of office procedures, or schedule five sales calls. Don't think about other tasks or responsibilities until the task at hand is completed.

Realize that as a Christian, God owns you and may see your plight differently from the way you see it.

The apostle, Paul, reminded the Corinthian Christians, "You are not your own; you were bought at a price." (I Corinthians 6:19-20) Jesus gave His life for us on the cross, not to make us comfortable in this world, but to prepare us to live for eternity in the next world. When Jesus was on the earth, He continually urged His disciples to raise their focus from the temporal to the eternal. To the Samaritan woman at the well Jesus said, "Everyone who drinks this water will be thirsty again, but whoever drinks the water I give him will never thirst. Indeed, the water I give him will become in him a spring of water welling up to eternal life." (John 4:13-14)

We need the eternal perspective because we are prone to get bogged down in earthly cares. The earthly cares are not invalid or unrelated to the eternal; indeed, they are a vital part of it.

For example, one day Jesus told His disciples to cross the Sea of Galilee in their fishing boat. After they set out, Jesus settled Himself comfortably on a cushion in the stern and went to sleep. A windstorm blew in from the Great Rift Valley and struck the sea with sudden fury. When the waves threatened to capsize the boat, the disciples knew they were in great danger. Indignant at Jesus' apparent indifference to their plight, they woke Him and demanded, "Teacher, don't you care if we drown?" (Mark 4:38) They had forgotten Jesus' last words to them, "Let us go over to the other side." (4:35) He did not say, "Let us go out to the middle of the sea and drown." The reason they were in the middle of the sea in a storm was their obedience to Jesus' instructions; but they only saw their situation in terms of fearful danger and potential disaster. Jesus saw it as a test of their faith and an opportunity to see His power at work. After He commanded the winds and the waves, "Quiet! Be still!" and calmed the sea, He asked, "Why are you so afraid? Do you still have no faith?" (4:39, 40)

When you face a difficult, frightening, or even dangerous circumstance, you are probably in it because God either caused or allowed it to happen for a spiritual purpose. "And we know that in all things God works for the good of those who love him, who have been called according to his purpose." (Romans 8:28) Daily happenings are important because they are opportunities for the eternal to impact your life.

Utilize faith plus works.

Although one of the ways worry can get a hold on us is lack of faith, faith alone is not necessarily the solution. "...Faith by itself, if it is not accompanied by action, is dead." (James 2:17) Worry will come back to haunt you if you try to dismiss a problem with the simplistic attitude, "God is in control. I'm not going to try to do anything about my problem. I'm just going to have faith that everything will turn out all right." That is putting faith in faith. It is not biblical faith.

Biblical faith says, "I am going to trust that God will guide and empower me to do something that will prove to be a solution to the problem that is worrying me." Of course, there are some problems that are beyond your control, but even then you can adjust your attitude or behavior in response to the problem.

Identify some of the factors in your daily life that are causing chronic stress. They could be bad eating habits, lack of exercise, poor management techniques, negative responses to significant people in your life, or an unrealistic, over programmed schedule. Select a couple and formulate a plan to eliminate them.

Before the days of power steering, it was extremely difficult to turn the wheels of an automobile when it was parked. But when it was rolling down the highway at some speed, it was easy to steer. God's guidance is somewhat like that. When you step out in faith—after much thought and prayer seeking God's guidance—and take some action, it is more likely that God will direct or redirect you than if you hold back and do nothing. It is easier to direct a moving object than to move a stationary one.

Be prepared as much as possible beforehand.

Certain kinds of stress can be avoided simply by making better decisions. If, for instance, you want to attend the 10 o'clock Sunday morning service, you will avoid much unpleasantness if you set the alarm clock early enough to allow plenty of time to dress, eat, and drive to the church. Arriving early will help reduce the likelihood of a stressful morning of worship. Planning ahead helps us maintain control over the areas of life that are ours to manage.

Of course, not all areas are ours to control, and stressful situations can happen through no fault of our own. You may arrive early at church with a pleasant smile on your face and a song in your heart only to learn that the person who was supposed to help you teach Sunday school is too sick to be there. The stress you feel at that point is beyond your control, but at least your early arrival gives you more time to formulate a plan for teaching the class alone.

Use Scripture as a weapon.

God has provided you with a veritable arsenal of weaponry to fight against the evil forces that come against you with stress and anxiety. "For the word of God is living and active. Sharper than any double-edged sword, it penetrates even to dividing soul and spirit, joints and marrow; it judges the thoughts and attitudes of the heart." (Hebrews 4:12)

If your life has gotten out of balance, the Bible will show you where you are wrong. Jesus quoted scripture to Satan when He was tempted in the wilderness. There is great power in God's word. Memorizing passages so that you will have them when you face challenges will provide you with a powerful weapon. Keeping your guidebook handy can combat the danger of losing direction in a fast-paced environment.

Learn the art of relinquishment.

Self-reliance has been a theme in this country since its inception. Emerson's essay by that title has had a great influence on the American worldview since he published it in 1841. Emerson offered an image of the autonomous self that is free from all limitation and constraint. Essentially, it is a concept of man as god.

There is a deeply rooted notion in our culture that we can control our destiny. In the business world this is often called a "can do" attitude. One hears comments like, "Don't take 'no' for an answer," and "Have faith in yourself." Healthy self-confidence is one thing, but these ideas have been taken to an extreme.

Any thinking Christian immediately recoils at the suggestion that man is god. However, the idea that limitations are bad seems to have captured our imaginations more successfully. This is manifested in our resentment and indignation when life becomes painful or disappointing. When we think we are entitled to a stress-free existence because we are trying to be obedient, we are falling prey to a lie of the culture.

What does the Bible say about man? "...For he [God] knows how we are formed, he remembers that we are dust. As for man, his days are like grass, he flourishes like a flower of the field; the wind blows over it and it is gone, and its place remembers it no more." (Psalm 103: 14-16) The passage contrasts man with the Lord's loving kindness, which is everlasting. It reminds us that His sovereignty rules over all. So much for freedom from limitations!

A wise Christian will learn to discern the limitations his sovereign God has placed on his life. A few are so basic that it might be helpful to mention them here. First, it is important to remember that we do not have control over other people's wills. We must respect the "otherness" of those around us. Accepting this reality enables true love to take place. If others were not truly separate entities from yourself you would never love anyone but yourself. Respect the rights of others to make choices in their own self-interest, but do not take responsibility for them yourself. You are responsible for your own decisions, including the way you respond to others when they make choices you don't like.

Secondly, we cannot eliminate the laws of nature. Your body will require nourishing food and sleep; there will be day and night; and gravity will pull things toward the earth. These facts might seem so self-evident that they do not need to be stated, but our culture actually opposes these limits. Through technology we have attempted to conquer these laws, but they still hold power over us. We may have found a way to shop at all hours as if time no longer is relevant, but during some of those hours it will still be dark outside. God set the laws of nature in motion and they are His to control, not ours.

Thirdly, it is essential to remember that we cannot control God. We have to accept His sovereign will in our lives. There is no formula of obedience that will force God to obey our will. We can always trust that He is who He says He is, but we are never free to tell Him who He has to be.

All of this is bad news if you are a narcissist who wants people, nature, and God Himself to be extensions of your own identity. As a Christian, these limitations are a relief. Think of it this way: Limitations mean that you have a lot less to worry about. Now that is good news!

Exercise.

We will discuss the value of exercise in a later chapter, but it is good to state its importance in this context. When you are feeling a build up of stress, physical exertion can be a great way to relieve tension. It actually releases endorphins into your bloodstream that elevate your mood. Also, your body can handle the physical demands of stress more efficiently when you are in good condition.

Set aside a limited amount of time in a day to deal with the things that tempt you to worry.

Thirty minutes to an hour is recommended. The object of this exercise is to keep the poison contained. Rather than allowing a fear to haunt your thoughts throughout the day, use this designated time to think constructively about the issue or situation. Whenever a worrisome thought occurs to you, tell yourself, "I will think about this later during the designated time for it." When the time comes, pray and ask the Lord to help you deal wisely with your fear, and steep yourself in reminders of who He is. Nothing is more comforting than to glimpse a loving face when you are hurting. How much more so when it is the face of God Himself!

Remember, it takes practice to change the bad habit of worry.

Do not get impatient with yourself for struggling with temptation in this area, but stay vigilant in resisting it. Bad habits can be overcome, and you are not alone in your struggle. Instead of merely trying to avoid worrisome thoughts, replace them with positive, wholesome ones. "Finally, brothers, whatever is true, whatever is noble, whatever is right, whatever is pure, whatever is lovely, whatever is admirable—if anything is excellent or praiseworthy—think about such things." (Philippians 4:8-9)

A golfer who has just taken up the sport has to think consciously about everything he does: his grip, his stance, the bend in his elbows, and the arc of his swing. But after he has been playing for a while, these actions become second nature, and he hardly thinks about them. That is what practice does for you.

Likewise, when you first decide to change your habit of worry, you will have to think consciously about turning your thoughts from fear to faith. But with enough practice, you will eventually do it without thinking about it. When you reach that point, the thoughts that used to worry you will actually build up your faith.

THE ANTIDOTE FOR WORRY

The antidote for worry is peace. The world cannot offer anyone such a precious gift. One need only turn on the news for a few minutes, and it will become painfully clear that our society is lacking any form of true peace.

The world tries to achieve peace through faulty means. One is to adopt a mood of passive indifference. But there is nothing healthy about killing off your active concern and emotional engagement with life. That is actually a form of death.

Paul said in Philippians 4:6-7, "Do not be anxious about anything, but in everything, by prayer and petition, with thanksgiving, present your requests to God. And the peace of God, which transcends all understanding, will guard your hearts and your minds in Christ Jesus." Paul was in prison when he wrote these words. But the book of Philippians is about joy and peace. His message stands out brightly against the backdrop of his life. He did not have to wait until his circumstances improved to find peace, because he had the antidote to worry.

Dr. Fowler defines peace as: a promise that no matter what happens or what decisions we are forced to make, deep down in our souls there can be sustaining confidence that God is in control, and in the end, He will make everything work out for our good and His glory. If you have this peace, you will stand out from the culture. The stress and difficulty in your life do not have to be the statement you make to the world. Like Paul, the true message of joy and peace will be all the more powerful when people see that your painful circumstances do not alter the truth you proclaim.

CHAPTER 7

Too Busy to Be Quiet

FUMING IN THE KITCHEN

An incident in the life of Christ illustrates how excessive busy-ness can spoil even our loving, devoted service to Him and distract us from doing the one thing that He desires most for us to do. It is the story of Martha and Mary recorded in Luke 10:38-42.

The great Jewish scholar, Alfred Edersheim, suggests that Jesus' visit to the home of Martha, Mary and Lazarus in Bethany may have occurred during the Feast of Tabernacles. If so, a tent or arbor of living tree limbs with their leaves still attached would have been set up as the primary living area in the home, most likely in the inner courtyard.[1]

It began as a pleasant affair. Jesus sat under the arbor with sunlight and shadows dappling all around him while everyone enjoyed the cool breezes of the fall season. At first, Mary, Martha and the rest of the family sat before Jesus and listened to Him teach. But Martha could not concentrate on what Jesus was saying because her mind was distracted by the elaborate preparations she had made for the meal she would soon serve her honored guests.

Apparently, she persuaded Mary to join her in the kitchen to finish cooking the meal. After helping her sister for a while, Mary must have slipped out of the kitchen and resumed her place at Jesus' feet, identifying herself as one of Jesus' pupils.

As time for the meal drew near, Martha became flustered and upset. Busy with many unfinished tasks, she began to make noise in the kitchen, perhaps hoping to catch Mary's attention and shame her into coming back to help with the cooking. Mary continued to focus her attention on the person and words of Jesus.

Finally, her frustration and resentment got the best of her, and Martha broke in on the teaching session, directing her irritation first at Jesus. "Lord, don't you care that my sister has left me to do the work by myself? Tell her to help me!" she insisted. Ironically, she addressed Jesus as "Lord" and then presumed to give Him an order. She also assumed that her sister, Mary, was creating a problem when in fact, Martha herself was the problem.

"Martha, Martha," the Lord answered, "you are worried and upset about many things, but only one thing is needed. Mary has chosen what is better, and it will not be taken away from her." Jesus' rebuke was loving and gentle. He recognized Martha's good motive—desiring to serve an enjoyable meal to Jesus and His disciples. His rebuke was aimed at Martha's agitation and excessive busy-ness resulting from her over programmed schedule. There simply was not enough time to prepare an elaborate meal and still have time left to listen to Jesus' teaching. Mary was the first to realize that a choice had to be made between the two; and Jesus commended her for choosing to sit at His feet and hear what He had to say to her.[2]

SPIRITUAL DISCIPLINES: WHAT THE CHURCH FORGOT TO REMEMBER

In the 21st century, there are more Christians like Martha than like Mary. They faithfully attend church, maybe even assume a leadership role. They are busy serving Christ and the community, so busy that they cannot concentrate on what Jesus is trying to teach them. Their demanding work schedule, compulsive leisure activities and unrealistic over programming leave little or no time for contemplating the person and words of Christ.

One of the first casualties of an excessively busy lifestyle is the ability to enjoy being alone and quiet, which is necessary to tune in to the spiritual lessons the Holy Spirit wants to teach us. Perhaps the best spiritual discipline to counteract excessive busy-ness is solitude and silence. Unfortunately, since the Protestant Reformation, evangelical Christians have by and large considered that discipline optional or unimportant.

The monastic movement eventually led to extremes that sought to earn God's favor by self-punishment and humiliation, especially in the 12th century and afterward. Protestants rightly rejected that unbiblical approach to life; but by emphasizing salvation by grace through faith alone the reformers unwittingly gave later generations the impression that spiritual disciplines are not necessary to live the Christian life. That the reformers themselves did not completely abandon the disciplines is apparent from one of Martin Luther's quotes, "I have so much to do today that I must spend several hours in prayer."

COME APART BEFORE YOU COME APART.

Jesus set an example regarding solitude and silence that we would do well to follow. The gospels record numerous instances when He withdrew from the crowds of followers, interrupting His teaching and healing ministry to be alone with His heavenly Father. Since only a relatively small number of Jesus' activities during His three-year public ministry are recorded, the frequent mention of His withdrawals strongly suggests that they were an integral part of His lifestyle.

The most notable withdrawals were associated with crises in Jesus' life. The first and longest occurred at the outset of His ministry. After John baptized Jesus and designated Him the "Lamb of God, who takes away the sin of the world!" (John 1:29) the Holy Spirit sent Jesus into the Judean wilderness where He remained alone and fasted for forty days. At the end of that time, Satan came to Him and tempted Him. Dallas Willard points out that the forty days of solitude and fasting were not part of the temptation, but spiritual training and preparation for it.[3]

The next major crisis was the death of John the Baptist. Jesus evidently regarded John's execution by Herod Antipas as a foreshadowing of the nation's rejection of Him, since they were closely associated. "When Jesus heard what had happened, he withdrew by boat privately to a solitary place." (Matthew 14:13)

The culminating crisis was Jesus' struggle in prayer in the Garden of Gethsemane the night of His arrest before the crucifixion on the next day. (See Matthew 25:36-46.) Jesus entered the garden with all of His disciples; but He left them except Peter, James and John to go farther into the garden. Finally, He asked His most trusted disciples to watch while He went off by Himself to pray.

Jesus also spent time alone before making important decisions. For example, when He chose the twelve disciples who would carry on the work He had started after His death, resurrection and ascension, "...Jesus went out to a mountainside to pray, and spent the night praying to God." (Luke 6:12)

Facing crises and decisions were not the only times that Jesus sought solitude. It was a routine part of His ministry. For instance, Jesus had worked a long day at Peter and Andrew's home. When He healed Peter's mother-in-law of a fever, word spread through the village. After sundown, everyone in the village showed up at the house, bringing all who were sick and demon possessed. Jesus spent much of that evening healing many of them and driving out demons. He had good reason to want a full night's sleep, but something else was more important to Him. "Very early in the morning, while it was still dark, Jesus got up, left the house and went off to a solitary place, where he prayed." (Mark 1:35) Luke records that this was a regular practice for Jesus. "Yet the news about him spread all the more, so that crowds of people came to hear him and to be healed of their sicknesses. But Jesus often withdrew to lonely places and prayed." (Luke 5:15-16)

It should be clear to every Christian that Jesus was setting an example for us to follow; yet we still miss the point. We rationalize that Jesus' behavior in the above instances does not apply to us because He was the Son of God performing miracles every day and fulfilling His role as our Messiah and Savior.

In fact, Jesus demonstrated how God intends for humanity to function in relationship with Him. The writer of Hebrews makes this point. Referring to Jesus as the Son of God, he wrote, "Since the children have flesh and blood, he too shared in their humanity...For this reason he had to be made like his brothers in every way, in order that he might become a merciful and faithful high priest in service to God..." (Hebrews 2:14, 17) If Jesus felt it was necessary to spend time alone with God the Father to manage crises effectively, make competent decisions and to carry out His God-given work, how can we expect to function adequately while neglecting that discipline?

ARE SILENCE AND SOLITUDE NECESSARY YO LIVE THE CHRISTIAN LIFE?

The answer to that question is both "no" and "yes." No, it is not necessary to practice the discipline of solitude and silence in order to become a Christian or to remain one. You can muddle through your whole life as a Christian wondering why you don't have the spiritual power, peace and joy of other Christians you regard as "super saints." You can remain in the spiritual state the apostle, Paul, called "worldly," that is, subject to the limitations of your human nature. In this context, the term does not necessarily refer to immoral behavior. It simply means that your way of thinking, attitudes and decision-making are patterned after human society and culture. When jealousy and quarreling broke out in the church at Corinth, Paul wrote, "Brothers, I could not address you as spiritual but as worldly—mere infants in Christ. I gave you milk, not solid food, for you were not yet ready for it. Indeed, you are still not ready. You are still worldly." (I Corinthians 3:1-3a) When addressing the church in Rome, he admonished along the same lines, "Do not conform any longer to the pattern of this world, but be transformed by the renewing of your mind. Then you will be able to test and approve what God's will is—his good, pleasing and perfect will." (Romans 12:2) Notice that abandoning your worldly way of thinking and behaving is a prerequisite to experiencing God's will for your life.

If you are determined to live the Christian life to its full extent, then you will inevitably be drawn to the discipline of silence and solitude. Jesus promised, "I have come that they may have life, and have it to the full." (John 10:10) Jesus makes an abundant, totally fulfilling Christian life available to every Christian; but it does not occur automatically. He invites you to "Take my yoke upon you and learn from me, for I am gentle and humble in heart, and you will find rest for your souls." (Matthew 11:29) As you follow Christ in discipleship He will guide you into the abundant victorious Christian life and the disciplines necessary to achieve it. The apostle, Paul, gave a similar exhortation to the Philippians. "Whatever you have learned or received or heard from me, or seen in me—put it into practice. And the God of peace will be with you." (Philippians 4:9)

It is unrealistic to expect to achieve anything worthwhile without putting effort, discipline and long hours of practice into it. For example, it would be ludicrous to expect to go to the Colonial golf tournament and play like Tiger Woods simply by buying a set of clubs with his name on them, wearing the same kind of clothes that he wears, and mimicking his stance and swing. He became the great professional golfer that he is by spending years as a pupil under a mentor and countless hours practicing and perfecting his techniques.

You enter the abundant Christian life by learning from the Word of God the principles and practices required, and incorporating them into your daily life. It doesn't happen all at once. It is a life-long process. You need guidance, inspiration and spiritual power to live the Christian life to the full. You get them from the Word; but remember, the Holy Spirit of God wrote the Word of God. It is the Holy Spirit who leads you into the truth of the Word.

No eye has seen, no ear has heard, no mind has conceived what God has prepared for those who love him—but God has revealed it to us by His Spirit. The Spirit searches all things, even the deep things of God. For who among men knows the thoughts of a man except the man's spirit within him? In the same way no one knows the thoughts of God except the Spirit of God. We have not received the spirit of the world but the Spirit who is from God, that we may understand what God has freely given us. This is what we speak, not in words taught us by human wisdom but in words taught by the Spirit, expressing spiritual truths in spiritual words. The man without the Spirit does not accept the things that come from the Spirit of God, for they are foolishness to him, and he cannot understand them, because they are spiritually discerned. The spiritual man makes judgments about all things, but he himself is not subject to any man's judgment: For who has known the mind of the Lord that he may instruct him? But we have the mind of Christ. (I Corinthians 2:9-16)

To receive this spiritual guidance and discernment, it is necessary to tune in to the Holy Spirit. How do you do that? The same way you tune in a Christian station on your radio. All the radio stations, Christian and secular, are broadcasting all of the time. The ether is a cacophony of voices and music of all varieties. If you put your radio's tuner on "search" mode you can hear them all, but only one at a time, because when you tune in one station you tune out all the others. To hear the Christian station you simply find its frequency and set your tuner to it.

Tuning in to the Spirit requires you to tune out all the competing voices and sounds that clamor for your attention all the time. Solitude and silence is the way you set your spiritual tuner to the Holy Spirit's wavelength, so to speak. It tunes out other voices and the torrent of information streaming into your mind almost constantly. For example, in America you probably are exposed to an average of 3,000 advertising messages every day.[4]

God refuses to shout down the competing voices. He waits for you to seek Him. This attribute of God is revealed in His promise to the Jewish exiles in Babylon. "'For I know the plans I have for you,' declares the Lord, 'plans to prosper you and not to harm you, plans to give you hope and a future. Then you will call upon me and come and pray to me, and I will listen to you. You will seek me and find me when you seek me with all your heart. I will be found by you,' declares the Lord…" (Jeremiah 29:11-14a)

THERE IS NO SOLITUDE IN A BEEHIVE.

Bees are communal creatures. They work together in the hive in almost constant contact with each other in a state of excitement and activity. Yet, even bees leave the hive as individuals and go out by themselves to gather nectar from flowers. Their lives are a balance between working alone and living in a community.

For a Christian, there needs to be a balance between living in community in almost constant contact with other humans and experiencing solitude when you commune with God and nourish your soul. Too much time in solitude makes you a recluse, of little benefit to society. Too much time in community and too little solitude leave you spiritually malnourished.

If you are like most Christians, you spend nearly all of your time in the beehive. You are in contact with your family in the morning from the moment you wake up. You watch the news, weather and traffic reports on television while preparing to leave for work. During the drive to work a barrage of lighted signs and billboards assaults your mind. You turn on the radio or CD player when you crank the car. At work you are interacting with your associates and customers all day or focusing on specific tasks. Another commute like the one in the morning brings you back to your family. Your time is divided between them and the television or surfing the internet. Finally you drop into bed exhausted. After a few hours of sleep your clock radio wakes you up and you repeat the whole process.

There is nothing inherently wrong with any of those activities. Most of them are good and wholesome. The problem is that they are out of balance. Something vital is missing from that lifestyle. Jesus rebuked the Pharisees for doing good things while neglecting more important concerns. "Woe to you Pharisees, because you give God a tenth of your mint, rue and all other kinds of garden herbs, but you neglect justice and the love of God. You should have practiced the latter without leaving the former undone." (Luke 11:42) Are you neglecting to find time for silence and solitude to pray and commune with God?

SOLITUDE: WHERE CAN YOU FIND IT?

Solitude is not easy to come by in 21st century Western culture; but most worthwhile endeavors are not easy. A good starting point is simply to make different choices whenever you are alone for a few minutes. If you are the first person to enter the kitchen in the morning, choose to leave the television or radio off while you prepare breakfast. If you drive to work by yourself, listen to the traffic and weather reports if necessary, and then turn off your radio. Use the time to pray (with your eyes open, of course) or meditate on a scripture verse you have memorized.

Cassie Findley used to feel compelled to maximize the time during her 20 minute commute to work by listening to motivational CDs, radio programs, or talking on her cell phone. When she decided to make the drive in silence, it was painful for her at first. Then she began to use the time to dream about goals and imagine projects she would like to accomplish, plan the new day or reflect on the events of the day, and to pray. Before long, she began to look forward to her 40 minutes of solitude every day.

Another way to find some time for solitude is to take a brown bag lunch to work occasionally and eat it by yourself in a quiet place, such as a bench in a park. Use the rest of your lunchtime to pray and meditate. Activities like these will not fulfill all your need for solitude, but they will point you in the right direction.

You can take a lesson from the tactics Jesus used to find solitude. Sometimes He arose early in the morning before daylight. Most people are still asleep then, so it is relatively easy to find a quiet place to be alone for a little while, maybe in the den of your own house or on the patio. It is not necessary or advisable to do this every day unless you are going to bed early.

Other times, Jesus sought out lonely places in wilderness areas—desert, in His case. A weekend outing to a state or national park, woodland or beach could afford good opportunities for solitude and silence. For safety, you should take a partner with you and stay within earshot of each other during your alone times. Some married couples might enjoy alternating solitude with silent times together. Dating couples could try this, too, but at that stage of the relationship the other partner's presence could be a distraction.

Jesus often referred to prayer made in a closet. Walk-in closets are in most recently built homes and apartments. With a little rearranging, a corner of the closet could be set up with a chair or kneeling bench and a good light source for reading the Bible.

By now you should have the idea. Be creative. See what you can come up with to provide a few minutes of silence and solitude for yourself.

Solitude: What do you do with it?

Now that you have found a place for solitude, you need a plan for using the time most effectively. The first thing you want to accomplish is to settle down. That usually takes at least ten minutes or longer. Think of what it is like to drive a car. When you are hurling down the highway at fifty to seventy miles per hour and then decide you want to stop, you have to allow some time for the car to decelerate. The same is true for your mind and spirit. When you are hurling through life at top speed and then decide to stop for solitude and silence, it takes some time to let the momentum of your thoughts and activities subside.

Your objective is not to make your mind go blank. That is a technique used by transcendental meditation, yoga and other practices of Eastern mysticism. They can lead to serious nega-tive spiritual consequences.

Keep your mind fully engaged. The purpose is to redirect your thoughts from the "many things" that are crowding your mind to the "one thing" that occupied Mary's attention—the Word of truth.

One effective way to turn your thoughts in that direction while you are settling down is to pay attention to nature. "For since the creation of the world God's invisible qualities—his eternal power and divine nature—have been clearly seen, being understood from what has been made, so that men are without excuse." (Romans 1:20) "The heavens declare the glory of God; the skies proclaim the work of his hands. Day after day they pour forth speech; night after night they display knowledge. There is no speech or language where their voice is not heard. Their voice goes out into all the earth, their words to the ends of the world." (Psalm 19:1-4a) God's fin-gerprints are all over nature.

If you just take the time to stop, look, listen and think, na-ture will point you to God. Listen to the wind in the trees, the birds singing. Look at the artful design of the trees, the lush green color of grass or the artist's palate of colors in the flowers. Smell the fresh air, the hint of pine or other scented plants. Jesus used this technique to teach His disciples about God's provision and remind them not to worry. "Look at the birds of the air; they do not sow or reap or store away in barns, and yet your heavenly Father feeds them. Are you not much more valuable than they? Who of you by worrying can add a single hour to his life?" (Matthew 6:26-27) The Bible is full of references to nature like this one. If you are not familiar with them, spend a few minutes with a Bible dictionary and read the articles on plants, animals, minerals, earth, sun, moon, stars, heavens, and so forth. Then when you observe nature you will remember some of the con-nections the Bible makes between nature and God. With a little experience, you may begin to make some inferences yourself.

If you do not have the opportunity to go outdoors, then you could start your solitude time with prayer, telling God about some of the things that are pressing on your mind and then ask Him to help you relax and focus on Him. Next read a passage from the Bible. If you start your time outdoors, then this would be a logical second step.

It is important that you do your homework. Select a passage that you have previously studied. Your pastor's sermon text from last Sunday or a reference from your last Bible study class would be good choices. Otherwise, choose a passage you have studied for yourself. Pay attention to the passage's context and historical setting. Be sure you grasp the meaning of key words and phrases. If you do not take these precautions, your thoughts are liable to go off on a tangent based on a misinterpretation of Scripture. "Do your best to present yourself to God as one approved, a workman who does not need to be ashamed and who correctly handles the word of truth." (II Timothy 2:15)

Read the passage through at least twice, then ask God to help you understand not only its meaning but how it should be applied specifically to your life. Turn the passage over in your mind. Try to remember instances in your past when this truth related to your experience. Were your actions consistent or inconsistent with the teaching of this passage? Imagine yourself doing something in the future that would put this teaching into play in your life.

If you will listen, God will make Himself heard. However, "Be careful not to let your emotions get in the way when you listen to God," Dr. Fowler warns. As a safeguard, don't make impulsive, life-changing decisions based on isolated, subjective factors. If you feel God is telling you to do something, be sure to validate the message by checking it against biblical truth in a broader context and discussing it with trusted friends who are in a position to be more objective.

Alternate meditation on the passage with prayer. Ask God to forgive you if the passage shows up your disobedience—if you have not already done so. If you have previously confessed that sin, thank God for forgiving you. Pray for His help and guidance to make changes or take action that would bring your life into conformity with this part of the Word. If it is a promise, thank God for giving it and ask Him to give you the faith to claim it.

There is practically no limit to the variety of ways you can use the time in solitude and silence. A good practice would be to spend much of the time in prayer. The model prayer that Jesus taught His disciples illustrates the basic elements of prayer. (See Matthew 6:5-15.)

WHAT DO YOU SAY WHEN YOU WANT TO PRAY?

1. Worship

"Our Father in heaven, hallowed be your name..."

The first element is worship. It could be broken down into other elements: praise, surrender and thanksgiving. We praise God for being who He is and for His mighty acts. Praise Him for being all-powerful, all-wise, kind, gracious, merciful, loving, patient, good, and just. Praise Him for creating the universe and making it beautiful; for sending Christ as our savior; for preparing a future home for us with Him in eternity. Those are just a few suggestions to give you the idea.

In the Old Testament, believers brought offerings to be sacrificed on an altar as their act of worship. In the New Testament, the apostle, Paul, admonished Christians to present themselves in surrender and service to God as their act of spiritual worship. "Therefore, I urge you, brothers, in view of God's mercy, to offer your bodies as living sacrifices, holy and pleasing to God—this is your spiritual act of worship." (Romans 12:1) In your prayer time, affirm your willingness to abandon your own desires and will in favor of doing God's will and serving Him. Be specific. Select an activity you do regularly that could be curtailed or abandoned to free up more time with your family or for devotional time. Surrender it to God.

Giving thanks to God is a natural, universal human responsibility. When Paul leveled his indictment against unbelievers, he held them accountable for failing to give thanks to their Creator. "For although they knew God, they neither glorified him as God nor gave thanks to him..." (Romans 1:21) As a believer, you naturally want to remember to thank God for all He has done for you. Thank Him for prayers answered and for prayer requests denied in His wisdom for a greater good. Thank Him for life, health, freedom, family, forgiveness, salvation, and every other good thing you can call to mind. "Every good and perfect gift is from above, coming down from the Father of the heavenly lights..." (James 1:17)

2. Purpose

> *"your kingdom come, your will be done on earth as it is in heaven."*

This part of the prayer is an extension of the attitude of worship. It is asking God to complete His plans to bring the whole earth into obedience to His will. Even now, in heaven, when God issues a command, angels and cherubim are ready to spring immediately into action to carry out their instructions. Besides God's presence, that is what makes heaven such a desirable place. Everything about it is exactly the way God wants it to be: perfect, good, glorious, infinitely satisfying.

As you submit your will to God, His rule begins to guide and bless your life. You are experiencing a sample of life in His kingdom. When Christ returns to set up His kingdom on earth, this prayer will be answered on a global scale. The apostle, John, had a glimpse of that glorious event in his prophetic vision. He wrote, "Hallelujah! For our Lord God Almighty reigns. Let us rejoice and be glad and give him glory!" (Revelation 6b-7a) Pray that God will use you in accordance with His will to accomplish His purpose for this point in time and for eternity.

3. Petition

> *"Give us today our daily bread."*

The essence of prayer is asking. Jesus taught His disciples to ask God for the things they needed to accomplish God's will for their lives. Those needs begin with the essentials for physical existence—food, clothing and shelter—and extend to anything else you need to accomplish God's will for your life. "His divine power has given us everything we need for life and godliness through our knowledge of him who called us by his own glory and goodness." (II Peter 1:3) All you have to do is ask in faith. This is not a blank check to satisfy your selfish desires, but a promise to meet your legitimate needs.

Notice that the model prayer limits the needs you should pray for to those of the current day. Since you live life one day at a time, you should only expect to receive what you need for that day. Tomorrow you can ask for additional needs if they occur. Of course, some of today's needs may relate to things in the future. Nevertheless, they are still a component of your needs today.

Petition includes intercession. We are to pray not only for ourselves, but also for our family, our brothers and sisters in church, our circle of friends, and finally the whole world. "And pray in the Spirit on all occasions with all kinds of prayers and requests. With this in mind, be alert and always keep on praying for all the saints." (Ephesians 6:18) "I urge, then, first of all, that requests, prayers, intercession and thanksgiving be made for everyone—for kings and all those in authority, that we may live peaceful and quiet lives in all godliness and holiness. This is good, and pleases God our Savior, who wants all men to be saved and to come to a knowledge of the truth." (I Timothy 2:1-4a)

4. Confession

"Forgive us our debts, as we also have forgiven our debtors."

Confession of sin on a regular basis maintains your fellowship with God. Sin breaks your fellowship with God. There will be times when you slip back into your old habits and the cycle of busy-ness addiction will begin again. The solution is to recognize what is happening and confess your failure to God. He will forgive you and give you the grace to restore balance to your life.

When you ask God for forgiveness, it is imperative that you come with a willingness to forgive those who sin against you. This is the only part of the prayer that Jesus took pains to explain. That indicates how important it is. Your forgiveness and fellowship with God depend on your forgiving others. Your relationship with God is secure regardless. He remains your heavenly Father because you are in Christ; but you will be out of fellowship with Him if you harbor an unforgiving spirit toward others. He will not tolerate your hypocrisy if you ask Him to do something you are not willing to do for someone yourself when it is within your power to do it.

5. Deliverance

"And lead us not into temptation,
but deliver us from the evil one."

You are engaged in a spiritual war. There are powers of darkness that conspire to thwart your efforts to live the victorious Christian life and overcome your busy-ness addiction. You are no match for them. Your only hope to escape their tempting snares is the guidance and protection of God.

As you pray and meditate, consider the activities you are involved in and the plans you are making. Are any of them questionable? Could they lead you away from God and His will? What has resulted in the past when you engaged in similar activities? Pray that God will guide you away from situations that will tempt you to compromise your faith and commitment to godliness.

As you struggle with busy-ness addiction, be especially aware of old friends, surroundings and activities that could restart the cycle of addiction. Ask God to help you steer clear of them as much as possible. When it is necessary to be in those circumstances, pray that God will give you the strength to keep your resolve to maintain the balance in your life.

• • • •

These are the basic elements of prayer. It would be helpful to memorize the model prayer and repeat it at the beginning of your prayer time. Just be sure to think about the meaning of the words every time you say it. Otherwise, it could become "vain repetition." Then think through the outline of the prayer and personalize it for the issues you are facing.

How do you get a daily time for solitude and silence started?

If you ever meet a member of the Navigators, he is almost certain to give you a booklet titled, "Seven Minutes with God" by Robert D. Foster. He suggests that you start with seven minutes for your quiet time: thirty seconds to pray for guidance, four minutes for Bible study, and two and a half minutes in more prayer.

You may think, "That doesn't seem like nearly enough time to do all of that adequately," and you would be right. The genius of Foster's method is that it starts you moving in the right direction. You cannot honestly say that you are not able to carve out seven minutes sometime during the day—even with a busy schedule—if you think something is important. You could set your alarm clock seven minutes earlier in the morning. Skip the second cup of coffee at breakfast or use one of your coffee breaks. Shave off seven minutes from your lunch hour. Skip a television program in the evening. If all else fails, take seven minutes before you go to bed at night.

After you get into the habit of spending seven minutes in solitude and silence every day, you will begin to enjoy it so much that you will want to extend the time. Seven minutes will grow to ten, then twenty or perhaps thirty. Occasionally, when your schedule permits, you might go for even longer periods, especially if you are facing a crisis or a big decision.

You will discover that spending time in solitude and silence when your schedule is already crowded is paradoxical. Rather than diminishing your effectiveness, time spent in solitude and silence taps resources of spiritual power and discernment that you were not utilizing, and enables you to make better use of the remainder of your time. The difference is that you are inviting

God to be more involved in your life, and you are aligning your-self with His purpose and will.

Every day you put off getting started, the less likely you are to get around to it. Where can you carve out seven minutes from your schedule today?

CHAPTER 8

Mirror, Mirror on the Wall... Who's That?

If you are too busy to plan and eat nutritious meals, then you are not living life at its optimum level. You are also setting up a vicious cycle. When you neglect your body's physical needs, it does not function the way God designed it to function. Your energy level drops; your ability to focus and act decisively fades. Even worse, you are more vulnerable to the effects of stress, and more likely to become anxious and depressed. An unhealthy body slows you down, so it takes more time to accomplish the same results than it would if you were healthy. You work longer and harder for fewer results. Your efficiency continues to decline, but your responsibilities and activities remain the same or even increase. It is a downward spiral.

YOUR BODY: A TEMPLE

Taking time to be healthy is more than a means to increase your efficiency. It is a spiritual responsibility. "Do you not know that your body is a temple of the Holy Spirit, who is in you, whom you have received from God? You are not your own; you were bought at a price. Therefore honor God with your body." (I Corinthians 6:19-20)

Although the context of this verse refers to sexual morality, there is a wider implication. The apostle, Paul, establishes a principle: the Holy Spirit dwells in the believer's body as the Spirit of God indwelt the Jerusalem temple in Old Testament times.

Solomon's temple was considered one of the wonders of the ancient world. According to the Jewish historian, Josephus, its upper chambers towered about one hundred eighty feet above ground level. The wooden roof was covered with marble, and the inside walls of the lower chamber were covered with cedar wood, beautifully carved in the shapes of angelic beings, palm trees, garlands and flower blossoms. The floors were covered with cypress wood. The walls, floors, and even the ceilings were overlaid with gold. The doors were made of cedar and olive wood decoratively carved, and hung on golden hinges. Two massive brass pillars flanked the entrance, and terraced courtyards surrounded the building.[1] It was truly a magnificent structure. God gave explicit and detailed instructions concerning its use and maintenance.

That our physical bodies have replaced the temple as the dwelling place of God on earth is a humbling thought. How we use and care for our bodies is not a matter of indifference to God. It is a solemn responsibility and stewardship that indicates our respect for the One who created them and deigns to dwell in them with us.

When Christ died on the cross, He redeemed not only our souls and spirits, but our bodies as well. To redeem means "to buy back." So, when you trusted Christ as your savior, the ownership of your body transferred from yourself to Christ. Now you are a steward—someone who takes care of someone else's property for him. That means you are accountable to the owner for the way you manage what belongs to him.

YOUR BODY: A LIVING SACRIFICE

Paul uses another similar but slightly different analogy to describe the relationship of the believer's body to Christ.

"Therefore, I urge you, brothers, in view of God's mercy, to offer your bodies as living sacrifices, holy and pleasing to God—this is your spiritual act of worship." (Romans 12:1) Although our bodies belong to God, we still have a choice in the way we use them. We can deny God's rightful ownership and misuse our bodies in ways that dishonor Him, or we can willingly offer our bodies to Him as a sacrifice.

Why should we do that? Paul says it is "in view of God's mercy." That was the underlying theme in the first eleven chapters in the book of Romans. We were all sinners in rebellion against God. We deserved death and destruction, but God in His mercy sent His Son to redeem us. "...for all have sinned and fall short of the glory of God, and are justified freely by his grace through the redemption that came by Christ Jesus. God presented him as a sacrifice of atonement, through faith in his blood." (Romans 3:23-25a) Just as God presented His Son as a sacrifice to pay for our sins, we should offer our bodies to serve and honor Him out of love and gratitude.

In the Old Testament days the priests placed the bodies of dead animals on the altar as a sacrifice to God. We are to present our bodies as a living sacrifice. The problem with a living sacrifice is that it keeps crawling off the altar. Maybe that has been your experience. Here are some suggestions to help you put your body back on the altar.

BALANCING THE BODY

There is an important difference between a Christian honoring God in his body and a New Age devotee's zealous conditioning of his own body or a narcissist's fascination with his body. The New Ager in the final analysis considers himself to be a god; so keeping his body strong and fit is a form of self-worship. The narcissist dreads the thought of aging and death, so he dedicates himself to fitness to delay the inevitable and to maintain the perfect image of himself. In both cases the focus is on the self.

As a Christian you will not care for your body for selfish reasons. You will do it to honor and worship God, to keep yourself fit for service to God and other people. You will probably eat a healthy diet and follow exercise regimens similar to the New Age practitioner or the narcissist, but with an entirely different attitude and motivation. You will not be driven by a frenzied god complex or fear.

Some Christians, especially those in ministry leadership positions, get out of balance by going to extremes in their service and devotion. Buying into the old heresy of asceticism, they imagine they are honoring God by ignoring the body's needs and focusing entirely on ministry. Remember, asceticism is not a biblical concept, but grew out of Gnostic dualism—the belief that the body is evil and only the spirit is good. They don't pay attention to what they eat, don't exercise consistently, don't get enough rest, and make no meaningful effort to relieve the stress in their lives. You know Christians who are like that. One of them is probably your pastor. Perhaps you are one of them.

Here Christians fall into a subtle trap laid by our adversary, Satan. Occasionally the evil one will seduce a Christian to fall into some moral failure and destroy his effectiveness for service to Christ; but those cases are exceptions. Most Christians and their leaders resist the temptation to commit sins that they know will destroy their ministries. However, it makes little difference to Satan whether a Christian's effectiveness is destroyed by sin or by misguided devotion. The result is the same.

The fact is, asceticism is not effective in the long run. Instead of promoting spirituality as it is supposed to do, it usually leads to emotional breakdown and moral failure, physical burnout and discouragement, or simply the inability to continue functioning effectively due to poor health.

When we are fatigued and malnourished we are less likely to make spiritual choices. Our natural tendency is to follow the course of the world, like a dead fish floating down a river. That is why the apostle, Paul, admonishes us, "Do not conform any longer to the pattern of this world, but be transformed by the renewing of your mind." (Romans 12:2) But it takes energy and will to swim upstream, that is, to go against the culture and implement choices based on spiritual principles from the Word of God. When we are tired we are not as resistant to temptation, resort to a defensive fight or flight response, tend to generalize when encountering difficulties, and are less visionary.

A biblical case in point is the story of Elijah. He had just experienced a dramatic victory over the priests of Baal in a confrontation at Mount Carmel. Afterwards, the evil Israelite queen, Jezebel, vowed to kill him. In an uncharacteristic response, Elijah panicked and fled for his life. Alone in the Judean desert under a broom tree, he gave in to despair. "I have had enough, Lord," he said, "Take my life. I am no better than my ancestors." (I Kings 19:4) Why was the great prophet of God so depressed? The next sentence gives a clue. It says that Elijah lay down and went to sleep. Evidently he was physically exhausted.

God heard Elijah's prayer and sent an angel to minister to him. Just a short time earlier Elijah had called down fire from heaven, but the angel gave no such spectacular divine assistance. Instead, he woke Elijah up and provided a simple meal of bread and water. Here is another clue to the reason for his depression. He was malnourished. After eating and drinking, Elijah went back to sleep. Later, the angel returned and repeated the meal a second time. Refreshed, Elijah abandoned his own deathwatch and resumed his journey. He traveled for forty days and forty nights to a cave in Mount Horeb.

But Elijah had still not recovered from his blue funk. All that time he had been traveling in the wrong direction, running away from the responsibilities God was giving him. "And the word of the Lord came to him: "What are you doing here, Elijah?" (I Kings 19:9) The clear implication is that God had not led him there. Later God would reveal that He wanted Elijah to go to Damascus, Syria.

Elijah's response to God's question shows how in his mind he was generalizing and exaggerating the obstacles he faced. He replied, "I have been very zealous for the Lord God Almighty. The Israelites have rejected your covenant, broken down your altars, and put your prophets to death with the sword. I am the only one left, and now they are trying to kill me too." Elijah's thinking bordered on paranoia. It was true that Israel was at a turning point in its history and was on the verge of abandoning Jehovah worship altogether. But it was also true that Elijah's success on Mount Carmel against the priests of Baal had turned the tide, at least for that generation.

It was also true that the queen, Jezebel, was trying to kill him, but Elijah generalized and said "they" were trying to kill him, as if everyone in Israel were against him. God corrected that distorted thinking by pointing out, "Yet I reserve seven thousand in Israel—all whose knees have not bowed down to Baal and all whose mouths have not kissed him." (I Kings 19:18)

Elijah had lost his vision. He did not expect that his victory at Mount Carmel would make a difference in the future of the nation, but it did. God had plans for Elijah to anoint kings in Syria and Israel. The anointing of Jehu as king over Israel would bring down the corrupt dynasty of Ahab and Jezebel and end the threat against Elijah's life. His anointing of Elisha as his successor would provide godly spiritual leadership to the nation for another generation. Elijah had painted his own dark version of Israel's future in his mind and lost sight of the God who could interdict and save.

Elijah was one of the greatest prophets; but he almost lost his ministry when he became physically exhausted and malnourished. Fasting for brief periods for a specific purpose is not harmful, but chronic neglect of your body's basic nutritional needs will lead to breakdown and failure. Here are some suggestions for insuring that your body gets the nutrients it needs for energy and maintenance of good health and a positive mental outlook.

BALANCING YOUR DIET

When you were in grammar school you were taught that you should eat a "balanced diet." If you are a "baby boomer" that meant choosing foods every day from the "Big Four" food groups: (1) breads, (2) meats and dairy products, (3) vegetables, and (4) fruits. Today most nutritionists group foods into six categories: (1) bread, cereal, rice and pasta (2) fruits, (3) vegetables, (4) meat, poultry, eggs, fish, beans, and nuts, (5) milk, cheese and yogurt, (6) fats, oils and sweets. The foods in these six groups fall into three broad categories: fats, proteins and carbohydrates.

THINK FATS

Fats have been given a bad "rap." You get the impression from advertising and product packaging that low fat or no fat is the way to go if you want to be healthy. Actually that is a gross oversimplification. Some fats are bad and should be avoided; and too much of anything can be harmful. But fat is an essential nutrient. Cassie Findley adds that eating the right amounts of the right kinds of fats plays a vital role in maintaining good health.

Perhaps that is why our Creator made fats taste so good. For example, if you are choosing a steak at the grocery store, pick the one with the best marbling, that is, the interspersing of fat and lean tissue. When cooked it will be juicy and flavorful, whereas a very lean cut will be relatively dry and almost tasteless. The breakdown of fat in your mouth sends a message to the pleasure center of your brain. It encourages you to load up on this calorie rich food. Your body needs calories to maintain its temperature and to produce energy for strenuous activity.

This affinity for fats is helpful in societies that only eat red meats occasionally, which still includes most of the world today. A problem arises in affluent developed nations where red meat is consumed nearly every day, and people work for their living in air-conditioned offices and plants doing tasks that require only small amounts of physical exertion. They don't need as many calories as people doing manual labor outdoors in all kinds of weather. The solution is to let your head determine how much fat you consume, not your taste buds. To do that, there are some things you need to know about fats.

BAD FATS

First, there are some fats that should be avoided. Most of these are the result of man-made refining processes. Pure fat is volatile and spoils easily. To stabilize it and make it easier to handle on its way from the farm to the distributor's warehouse to the store shelves and finally to your home, various methods are used. One of the most popular among food producers is hydrogenation: adding hydrogen to the molecules of unsaturated fats. A prime example is margarine, but if you read food product labels carefully you will find partially hydrogenated fats in many other products such as peanut butter, vegetable shortening and fried potato chips.

There are several good reasons to avoid hydrogenated oils. One is that the process requires a catalyst consisting of nickel and aluminum. Remnants of these metals survive the process and remain in the food. There is mounting evidence that associates aluminum with Alzheimer's disease, osteoporosis (bone deterioration) and even cancer.[2]

Another reason is the many ways hydrogenation changes the chemical composition of fats and their effect on the body. Almost all of the known effects are negative. For example, a study by the *New England Journal of Medicine* in 1990 found that trans-fatty acids produced by hydrogenation increase cholesterol levels in the body, including the "bad" LDL form (low density lipoprotein). High levels of LDL can increase the amount of plaque in arteries, an important factor in cardiovascular disease.[3] Even more disturbing is the fact that there are literally thousands of possible chemical reactions that occur during hydrogenation, but only a few of them have been studied and evaluated. For most of these reactions the potentially harmful effects remain unknown. As of this writing the Food and Drug Administration is planning to require that trans-fats be listed on food product labels. Also, a panel from the National Academy of Sciences' Institute of Medicine stated in a report released in the summer of 2002 that trans-fats should be avoided entirely in the diet because they have no known nutritional value and there is no safe level of consumption.[4]

Another fat to avoid is cooking oil that has been subjected to high heat, especially if heated for prolonged periods of time. Subjecting oils to heat, light and oxygen produces free radicals and polymers—combinations of two or more molecules of a simpler substance—not naturally found in food. Nothing good for your health can come out of that combination. For example, the chemical acrylamide, a suspected cause of cancer, has recently been discovered by scientists in Sweden in fried food and food baked at high temperatures.[5] Unfortunately, cooking oil used in many commercial deep-frying operations remains heated and exposed to light and oxygen for days at a time.[6] How long do you think they keep the oil hot in your favorite fast-food restaurant, and how often do you think they replace it with fresh oil?

GOOD FATS

On the other hand, most fats are beneficial. Collectively called triglycerides, they perform many useful functions. One is to insulate your body. Without a layer of fat, your body would require the generation of more heat, increased food consumption, more resources devoted to digestion and absorption of food. Imagine how much extra electricity your hot water heater would consume if you set it out in your garage and removed the insulation from the storage tank.

Body fat is also a cushion for your body. If it weren't for a layer of fat, you would bruise or possibly damage your body severely every time you bump into something. The fat in your heels absorbs some of the shocks from walking and running. Most important, fat tissues serve as reservoirs to store energy until your body needs it.

In addition, your body converts potentially toxic excess sugars in the blood into triglycerides, which are less harmful. They are protective mechanisms for the body.

Eating too many fried foods has thrown the average American's fat consumption out of balance. Not only do we tend to eat too many fats, we also eat too much of omega-6 fatty acids and not enough omega-3s. Omega-6 is the fat in most cooking oils and omega-3 is in dark green leafy vegetables, soy beans, walnuts and flax seeds as well as certain cold-water marine fish. A one-to-one ratio of omega-6 to omega-3 is generally considered normal and desirable, since both are useful to the body.

However, estimates of ratios in the typical Western diet frequently run as high as 10:1 and 25:1, and in extreme cases even 40:1. That is too much of a good thing, and can contribute to metabolic imbalances, inflammation, plaque formation in the arteries and heart disease.

Another good thing we tend to get too much of is saturated fats. These are the fats that are solid at room temperature, such as the fat in red meat. They are easily digested and useful for energy. In the intestines some feed beneficial bacteria and others suppress the growth of harmful bacteria such as candida and yeasts. Still others form cell membranes throughout the body. When excessive amounts of certain saturated fatty acids are eaten in combination with too many carbohydrates, they cause blood platelets to become sticky and may contribute to heart and circulatory disease. That is why we should not eat too much of them.

PLANTS DO IT

Triglycerides store essential fatty acids (EFA). The Human body can either manufacture or convert something else into the fats it needs, except for EFAs. Only plants can manufacture them. That is why they are "essential" to your diet.

EFAs perform vital functions in the body. They are involved in the process of oxidation, the "burning" of food by the body to produce the energy it needs for the process of living. They also are responsible for transferring that energy throughout the body.[7] By suppressing chemicals produced when your body is under stress, such as cortisol and norepinephrine, they help the body cope with chronic stress. Since they form a critical part of all cell membranes, including nerves, they are important to healthy brain function. For example, a deficiency in DHA—one of the EFAs—during infancy has been linked to attention-deficit-hyperactivity disorder.[8] In adults, inadequate amounts of DHA can result in increased aggression, depression and other behavioral disturbances.

These are just a few of the reasons why the current low fat/ no fat diet fads that do not distinguish between good and bad fats are not good for you, and can actually be harmful to your health. Good fats when balanced with proteins and carbohydrates keep your body functioning at its optimum level.

PROTEIN: THE NEGLECTED NUTRIENT

Protein in American diets is like the proverbial baby that gets thrown out with the bath water. Because of their tendency to eat too much red meat containing saturated fats, Americans have resorted to a relatively low protein high carbohydrate diet. This is the diet recommended by the Food and Drug Administration, athletic trainers and the American Dietetic Association until recently. The next time you are out in a crowd at a shopping mall or a sports stadium look at the people around you. It is a good bet that the vast majority of them are overweight. It should be obvious even to the casual observer that something is very wrong with the average American's diet. One of the problems is an inadequate amount of the right kinds of protein in proportion to the other macronutrients: fats and carbohydrates.

YOUR BODY: IT'S NOT WHAT IT USED TO BE

Protein performs many functions in the body. It is a source of energy, and plays a role in the production of hormones, enzymes, red blood cells and antibodies (disease fighting globulins). But protein's most important function is the building and rebuilding of tissue. All the cells in your body become worn out and must be replaced. For example, skin cells only last about one month, and the cells that line your digestive tract need replacement about twice every week. When you have been injured or sick, your body needs extra protein for the healing process. In short, your body cannot remain strong and healthy without adequate protein.

THE BEST SOURCES OF PROTEIN

Foods contain two kinds of protein: complete and incomplete. The key ingredients in proteins are amino acids. Some of them are called "essential" because the body cannot synthesize them. They must be supplied by the food you eat. Complete proteins contain all the essential amino acids. You get them from meat, fish, poultry, cheese, eggs and milk. Incomplete proteins do not contain all the essential amino acids. They include grains, beans, peas, peanuts and green leafy vegetables.

While it is true that combining incomplete proteins like beans and rice can produce a complete protein, the best source is animal products. One reason is that the fiber in vegetables inhibits the absorption of amino acids. Animal protein has no fiber. Another reason is the ratio of protein to calories. For example, a small serving of grilled chicken breast contains 28 grams of complete protein and 172 calories. You would have to eat almost four cups of cooked rice and one cup of navy beans to get that much protein (assuming you could absorb it), and you would also consume about 580 calories with it.[9] The protein requirement of the average male is approximately 75 to 80 grams per day. It would be difficult to get that much complete protein from vegetables without consuming far too many calories in the process, especially if you eat a balanced diet that also includes fats and fruits. That is why a vegetarian diet is likely to provide either too little protein or too much carbohydrate or both.

CARBOHYDRATES: THE GOOD, THE BAD AND THE UGLY

Carbohydrates play a vital role in the diet. Along with fats, they are a major source of fuel for your body's energy needs. Glucose from carbohydrates is the fuel that fires up your brain. Without an adequate supply, your thinking becomes "foggy." In addition, carbs are a major source of micronutrients such as vitamins, enzymes and minerals that are essential to good health.

The best carbohydrates are called "complex." That means their molecular structure consists of long chains of sugar units bound up in a single molecule. They must be broken down to produce glucose, and that process slows their entry into the bloodstream. Fiber content is also important. Besides keeping the bowels clean and functioning regularly, fiber slows the absorption of glucose into the bloodstream. Broccoli, for example, is a high fiber complex carbohydrate.

Simple carbohydrates are easy to detect because they taste sweet. A couple of examples are refined sweeteners such as cane or beet granulated sugar and corn syrup. These carbs create problems because they contain no fiber and enter the bloodstream very rapidly. Soft drinks and candies are loaded with them.

More important than the amount of sugar in food is the rate at which the sugar enters the bloodstream. Nutritionists call this rate the glycemic index. Carbohydrates with a high glycemic index enter the bloodstream very quickly. When sugar enters the bloodstream faster than the body can burn it for energy, the blood sugar level becomes elevated. Excess blood sugar has a toxic effect because of its high oxygen content. Not only does it create a favorable environment for free radical damage, it also oxidizes LDL cholesterol and turns it into plaque.

Plaque build-up is a major cause of heart disease. For years doctors have blamed plaque formation on the presence of cholesterol in the blood; but excess sugar is the real culprit. LDL does not form plaque unless it comes into contact with excess sugar.[10]

Your pancreas responds to excess blood sugar by secreting the hormone, insulin. Insulin converts the excess sugars into triglycerides (fatty acids) and stores them. A small amount goes into the liver and muscle tissue and the rest goes into adipose (fat) tissue. So, you are not likely to get fat by eating fats; you get fat mainly from eating too much of high glycemic carbohydrates. What is worse, as long as you continue on a high carbohydrate diet, insulin prevents most of the fat in the adipose tissue from being released, even if you exercise vigorously. The result is that you stay fat.

Unfortunately, your body does not restore perfect balance right away. After the insulin reaction sets in, the blood sugar level usually drops below normal. When that happens, you feel sluggish, lose some of your mental sharpness, and crave more carbohydrates to kick up your blood sugar level again. The residual insulin in your blood prevents the glucose from being released from your liver, so the only way you can turn off the

alarm signal in your glucose-starved brain is to eat more carbohydrates. Then your blood sugar level shoots up again, trigger-
ing another insulin response. You are caught in a vicious cycle.

Admittedly, about 25% of the American population does
not have this problem with insulin sensitivity. They were
blessed when their genetic codes were formed; so they can eat
whatever carbohydrates they want with few noticeable consequences. On the other hand, another 25% of the population
suffers acutely from this problem. The rest of us experience
it in varying degrees.[11]

HORMONAL HORRORS

Bouts of low blood sugar symptoms and weight gain are bad
enough; but they are only part of the problem created by eating
too much high glycemic food. Gyrating hormone levels create
imbalances that damage your whole body.

God created the human body to work as a harmonious, deli-
cately balanced system. David wrote, "I praise you because I am
fearfully and wonderfully made…" (Psalm 139:14) Unfortunately, it has become fashionable to refer to naturally occurring
substances in the body as "good" and "bad." For example, HDL
cholesterol is considered "good," and LDL cholesterol is considered to be "bad." Hormones are categorized the same way.

The underlying presupposition seems to be belief in evolution. If man is simply the highest form of animal life to evolve
so far, then it is to be expected that some of his body parts and
functions have not been perfected. They may eventually prove
to be either evolutionary dead-ends or so-called vestigial organs
that have outlived their usefulness.

One who believes man was created by the almighty and om-
niscient God understands that the human body as God made it
was good and perfect (see Genesis 1:31). Sickness and disease
are the results of man's fall into sin and the ensuing curse (see
Genesis 3:14-19). Man continues to make choices that are not
in his body's best interest. Many of them create imbalances in
the body's natural functions, and are the primary causes of most
sickness. Man's choices affect not only the individual, but also

the environment in which he lives. Creation of toxic wastes, soil depletion, use of chemical pesticides, food additives and refining methods are other ways man undermines his own health.

It is inaccurate to suggest that any of man's health problems result from imperfections in the basic design of his body. So, there are no bad hormones. They all have a useful function. Bad things happen when something throws them out of balance with each other and the rest of the body.

The latest research has shown that hormones work in tandem with each other. Insulin, for example, works with glucagon to regulate the blood sugar level. When insulin knocks the blood sugar down to below the normal level, glucagon will eventually trigger release of sugar stored in the liver and bring the level back to normal. However, it usually takes several hours for the insulin level to subside, and you have probably drunk the soft drink or eaten the candy bar long before that happens.

In the meantime, the insulin has been doing things in your body that you would rather it didn't. Hormones travel from the organs that secrete them through the bloodstream, but they do not act directly. Rather, they produce secondary substances called eicosanoids that act on the cellular level. Various enzymes control their activity like a thermostat controls whether your air conditioning system turns on or off. Insulin breaks down through a series of reactions that eventually produce arachidonic acid. It in turn can produce certain prostaglandins and leukotrienes that cause inflammation, pain, and in some cases fever and other responses related to the body's immune system and survival responses. Although this response causes great discomfort, it can save your life when a disease invades your body.

However, you should not subject yourself to inflammation just for the pleasure of eating a 12-ounce beefsteak and a whole baked potato with Texas toast. You see, the enzymes that control this inflammation response react to the food you eat. If you eat too much high glycemic food at one meal or simply consume too many calories at once, you can trigger this inflammation response.

Also, you can eat too much of the foods that already contain arachidonic acid, such as beef, lamb, pork, egg yolks and dairy products. Theoretically, your body will compensate by producing less arachidonic acid when you ingest food containing it. But if your body chemistry is already tipping the scales toward the formation of arachidonic acid, and you consume relatively large amounts of it in your food as well, your body might not compensate sufficiently. Then you will suffer from chronic inflammation, such as headaches and arthritis.

SHOOTING WARS AND DIET WARS

Lately there has been much talk about "fad diets." That terminology is somewhat misleading. The word "diet" means the kind and amount of food prescribed for a person. Western culture has been prescribing a habit of eating that is perhaps the most widespread and longest lasting "fad diet" in all of history. Unless you choose an alternative way of eating, you will probably eat the way most of the other people in your culture eat. The hurried lifestyle, social pressure and media hype all work together to program your eating habits. The "diet" basically consists of too much red meat, altered fatty acids, too much of w-6 oils and too little of the w-3 oils, and insufficient vitamins, minerals and fiber, due to over consumption of refined foods.[12] It can be called a "fad" because it originated in the 19th century with the industrial revolution.

Before then, only wealthy people could afford to eat red meat every day. Refined foods such as white flour processed by hand-sifting methods were expensive. "Common" people had to be satisfied with "common" food, consisting mainly of whole grains, vegetables, fish and fowl. For them red meat was a delicacy rarely if ever enjoyed. The wealthy ate diets consisting almost exclusively of red meats and fatty, sweet pastries. As a result, their privileged status brought along with it arthritic gout and other degenerative diseases.

Napoleon Bonaparte played a major role in changing that arrangement. Because of the need to preserve and transport food over long distances to supply his huge army, he commissioned his suppliers to find a way to mass-produce refined flour cheaply. (Insects cannot live in or feed on white flour. That should tell us something.) After the Napoleonic wars, the new technology developed for Napoleon and his armies became available to the general public, and everyone could enjoy the "benefits" of refined flour and eventually sugar as well.

The rest is history. Obesity and the degenerative diseases that had been confined to a small wealthy class spread throughout the general population. Companies manufacturing processed foods used part of their hefty profit margins to advertise their products in the developing mass media. As Western society prospered from the industrial revolution, the average family could afford to eat red meats regularly.

After World War II America became the wealthiest industrialized nation in the world. Following the same diet as the rest of Western civilization, Americans inherited the health problems that accompanied it. As Americans became fatter and sicker, many of them began to search for a new diet plan that would help them lose weight and improve their health. This quest has produced varied approaches to diet. Each of the more successful ones has made some contribution to the improvement of the American diet. To save you the time it would take to sort through and try out the various approaches to dieting, here is a summary of the recent history of dieting. Examples were selected from the myriads of diets available to illustrate some of the most popular approaches to dieting.

PRITIKIN THE PIONEER

Nathan Pritikin was not a doctor or a researcher. He was an engineer with a diseased heart in the 1950s. Desperately searching for a solution to his own health problem, he proposed an idea that was considered strange and new in its day. He suggested that dietary habits are responsible for many of the most widespread diseases. If that were the case, then the best way to treat them would be with diet modification, not drugs. In spite of opposition from scientists and doctors, by the mid-1960s he had cured his heart ailment by exercising, eating a diet low in fats, and limiting carbohydrates to complex, high fiber foods that fill the stomach without adding too many calories to the diet. He also advocated eating frequent smaller meals.

His methods are still used today, and are particularly helpful to people suffering from cardiovascular disease. Some nutritionists are concerned that his diet might cause other health problems after the initial period of weight loss is over because it does not include sufficient amounts of some essential fatty acids, and could lead to deficiencies in fat-soluble vitamins over time.[13]

MAINSTREAM DIETS: CALORIE COUNTING

As concern grew over rising rates of obesity in America, researchers and doctors devised weight-loss diets. The consensus was that to lose weight, you simply must burn more calories than you consume. This can be achieved by doing two things in combination: (1) get more exercise, and (2) consume fewer calories than you burn.

This basic premise is an incontrovertible fact. However, implementing the strategy is extremely difficult for most people. Getting more exercise is not a major problem. If it is an activity you enjoy, such as swimming, jogging, working out in a health club, walking or gardening, just a modicum of discipline will make it a habit that becomes part of your lifestyle. The greatest problem is controlling the consumption of calories.

First, you have to keep track of what you are eating throughout the day, and look up the caloric content of the food you are about to eat. There are many variables that affect the caloric content of food, including the way it is prepared. For example, the kind and amount of oil used and the caloric content of various ingredients used in recipes must be determined and added to achieve an accurate result. That can be particularly difficult to do in a restaurant where you do not know how the food is prepared or what is in a recipe. But that is not the most difficult problem.

If you are simply counting calories, you must stop eating when you reach your quota. That point most likely will not coincide with the satisfaction of your hunger. You must exercise discipline to restrain the natural impulse to continue eating and be content to remain hungry after the meal is over. Most people can do that for a period of time if they are highly motivated to lose weight for a specific goal such as a wedding or a summer vacation at the beach; but the people who can voluntarily live with hunger every day for the rest of their lives are rare. Sooner or later, most calorie counters give up the diet, gaining back all the weight they lost and often even more.

ATKINS THE REVOLUTIONARY

Dr. Robert C. Atkins revolted against the calorie counting consensus of his colleagues and the low fat approach of Pritikin, proposing a radically different approach to diet in 1972 with the publication of his first book. He identified excess carbohydrate consumption as the primary cause of obesity. His diet allows you to eat practically as much as you want of proteins and fats, as long as you restrict the amount and kinds of carbohydrates in your diet. It advocates eating nutrient dense high fiber carbohydrates, such as broccoli. Although you begin with a severe restriction of carbs your first week (only 20 grams per day), you gradually increase their consumption until you achieve the desired weight level. Then you remain on a high protein, high fat, low carbohydrate diet for the rest of your life. The underlying assumption is that you will burn up the fats you eat for energy if you are eating only a few carbohydrates.

The Atkins philosophy of eating has many advantages. It discourages the consumption of highly refined carbohydrates like white flour and sugar. People who follow it definitely lose weight and keep it off as long as they stay on the plan. That is not overly difficult to do because you can eat big, hearty, flavorful meals with plenty of fat to give you energy and a feeling of satisfaction and fullness after each meal. The high fat content corrects the main drawback to the Pritikin diet (if weight loss is the objective and not treatment of cardio-vascular disease).

There are some concerns about this approach, however. It allows for the over-consumption of red meat and the saturated fats it contains, not to mention arachidonic acid. This raises a question about the probability of heart disease in the long run. The uncontrolled portion size allows for excessive calorie intake at a single meal, which can contribute to an inflammatory response. The low consumption of carbohydrates might not provide enough vitamins, minerals and other phyto-nutrients needed for optimum health. The Atkins diet tries to compensate with supplements, but whole foods are still the best source.

Finally, the low carbohydrate approach alters body chemistry, producing a state called ketosis. It is the body's natural way to manage starvation by burning stored fat instead of sugar for energy. It produces solvents called ketones in the process of breaking down fats for use by the body. One of them is acetone, which used to be the main ingredient in fingernail polish remover.

Some physicians are concerned that a prolonged state of ketosis could lead to health problems, but there is no evidence to that effect. A healthy body will simply flush the ketones out in the urine or breathe them out through the lungs with no apparent ill effects. However, some nutritionists think your brain will function sluggishly on ketones, since it is designed to burn glucose.

One thing is clear, however. Going on a low carbohydrate diet is like riding a tiger. The ride is thrilling, but if you ever get off, the tiger can attack you. Your body becomes extremely efficient in the use of nutrients when in ketosis. You could gain weight rapidly if you suddenly get off the program and resume eating a typical high carb diet. It is designed to be a lifetime commitment to a way of eating.

The Scarsdale Diet

In 1978, Herman Tarnower, a doctor in Scarsdale, New York, published *The Scarsdale Medical Diet* with Sam Sinclair Baker. Like the Atkins diet, it is high in protein and low in carbohydrates. The difference is that it is also low in fat. The meal plans are strictly laid out for you with little allowance for variation, so there is no counting calories or grams of fat. There is also no limit on most portion sizes, so hunger is not a problem immediately after meals. It advises you to cut out refined sugar and white flour. An aggressive weight-loss program, it aims at losing as much as one pound per day. Those who follow the program declare, "It works!"

Unfortunately, it is too good to be true. Of all the popular weight-loss programs, this one seems to be open to the most criticism. First, if you take weight off rapidly, you put it back on almost as rapidly if you deviate from the diet. Second, it has the same problem as Atkins with low carbohydrates, but to a greater degree: inadequate levels of fiber, vitamins and minerals. Between-meal snacking is limited to celery and carrots, so hunger can be a problem between the three meals per day allowed. Also, eating carrots as a snack by themselves does not consider the glycemic response and the inflammation it can cause. Third, it has the same problem as Pritikin with low fats: inadequate levels of essential fatty acids and other fats. It eliminates most dairy products. In short, you will most likely lose weight with this diet, at least for a while; but it could be at the expense of your good health.

THE U.S.D.A.'S FOOD PYRAMID CRUMBLES

To discourage the over-consumption of red meat and its accompanying saturated fats and to promote eating a balanced healthy diet, the U.S. Department of Agriculture published the "Food Pyramid" in 1992. It encouraged Americans to eat more grains, rice and pasta (6-11 servings per day), as well as vegetables (3-5 daily servings) and fruits (2-4 daily servings). Meat, poultry, fish, beans, eggs and nuts (2-3 servings daily) as well as dairy products (2-3 servings daily) were placed near the top of the pyramid. Fats, oils and sweets should be eaten "sparingly" and capped the pinnacle of the pyramid.

If reducing obesity in America was a goal of the pyramid, then it appears to have failed. The general consensus is that two thirds of Americans are overweight and one out of five is clinically obese. K. Dunn Gifford, spokesman for the non-profit organization, Oldways, in Boston blames this development on the pyramid.[14]

Defenders claim that the pyramid has not been tried and found wanting; it has not been tried at all by most Americans. Restaurants and advertisements by cereal companies have encouraged us to eat more grains, rice and pasta, emphasizing the bottom of the pyramid. Soft drink, pastry and candy bar manufacturers, on the other hand, glamorize the quick energy and pleasure gained from the consumption of their products, emphasizing the top of the pyramid. Vegetables and fruits don't have many advocates on Madison Avenue, so the middle of the pyramid gets short shrift in the typical diet.

While there is truth in that argument, there is growing concern among some doctors on the cutting edge of nutrition research that the U.S.D.A. food pyramid is out of date, and is not supported by the latest scientific findings. One of them is Dr. Walter Willett of the Harvard School of Public Health. He stated in an interview with ABC News on January 9, 2003, that there are several problems with the pyramid as it now stands. One is that it suggests all fats are bad and should be avoided for the most part. That ignores the importance of "good fats" in the diet. Another is the lack of distinction between refined grains like white rice, white flour—including pasta made from it—and their whole-grain counterparts, which are much healthier. Finally, he suggested that the U.S.D.A. might have a conflict of interest because of its close association with American agribusiness.[15] He recommended that the responsibility for constructing a diet guide for the American people be given to the National Institutes of Health or perhaps a non-governmental organization.

Dr. Willett has already started the ball rolling in that direction. He has constructed his own version of a dietary guideline pyramid in his book, *Eat, Drink and Be Healthy*. Based on several large studies conducted at Harvard University, his new "Healthy Eating Pyramid" focuses on the importance of individual foods in the diet instead of lumping them together in broad categories. It does not require weighing food servings or calorie counting. Rather, it is a lifestyle for eating that you can follow for the rest of your life.

BARRY SEARS AND "THE ZONE"

A former staff member at Massachusetts Institute of Technology, Barry Sears, Ph. D., has written several books advocating a similar approach to diet and nutrition. His main idea is that 40% of calories in the diet should come from carbohydrates, 30% from protein, and 30% from fats. Although this is not a radical departure from the allocation in the U.S.D.A. food pyramid or the diet recommended by the American Dietetic Association, the difference has been enough to stir up controversy. It increases the consumption of protein and decreases the consumption of carbohydrates. Sears' allocations are more moderate than those of Atkins and his predecessors.

His approach is individualized. The first step is to determine your own daily protein intake need, a simple do-it-yourself process described in his books. Then you eat three main meals and two snacks per day, being sure to go no longer than four or five waking hours without eating. The goal is to keep your blood sugar level within a comfortable "zone," avoiding either highs or lows that trigger hormone responses.

The meals and snacks all conform to the 40/30/30 ratio between carbohydrates, protein and fats. This part of the plan further moderates blood sugar levels and helps to avoid inflammatory responses. His books describe how to recognize "units" of the three macronutrients to determine portion sizes and individual food selections. Once you become familiar with the information about serving sizes you can use the "eyeball" method to choose your portions.

This is one of the first diets to take the glycemic index into consideration. Contrary to what some of his critics claim, Sears does not forbid eating high glycemic foods. He does alert you as to which ones they are and insists that you calculate their impact on the 40/30/30 ratio in the total meal. For example, if you are enjoying a dinner party with some friends and the entrée includes a large baked potato, you could still enjoy the potato if you want to; but you would have to limit your portion to less than a half-cup to remain in "the zone."

The "zone" is also more than just another diet. It is a plan for eating that you can use for life. It avoids most of the problems associated with other diet plans because it is more balanced. For example, it is not high protein; it simply aims for "adequate" protein. It is not high fat, but it is moderately low fat, emphasizing the consumption of healthy fats in moderation. It is not low carbohydrate, but avoids the problems created by over-consumption of them.

The strength of this plan is indicated by the criticisms leveled against it. None of them can point to any serious ill effects from following it. Some critics suggest that there is little research to support its presuppositions about hormonal responses to food. Actually, these concepts have been under study at Harvard University for the last ten years. Researchers have finally reached the point of making some conclusions from their studies. Their findings are beginning to be noticed by the general public, and a growing body of information is supporting their conclusions. There is not a massive body of research information yet because it is a relatively new development.

Another criticism is that the weight lost with this program is mostly water. That criticism could be made against any weight loss program for the first few pounds. However, the number of pounds people report losing and the trimming down of body fat cannot be attributed to water loss alone.

Similarly, it has been pointed out that people lose weight on the plan because it is low in calories. That simply states a truism. The only way anyone ever loses weight on any plan is to consume fewer calories than they burn. The important point is how that goal is achieved. "The zone" is a plan that helps you achieve that goal without counting calories or going hungry. By taking into account the glycemic index, it also helps you avoid the ill effects of both low and high blood sugar levels as well as various inflammatory responses.

Finally, some accuse Dr. Sears of telling people to stop eating some foods that are good sources of nutrition, such as carrots and bananas. As indicated above, "the zone" plan does not do that. It recommends reducing the portion size of high glycemic foods and eating them in combination with protein and fats that slow absorption of their sugar content. Also, "the zone" is not as strict as other plans. You are allowed to deviate from it up to 25% of the time, so no nutritionally beneficial foods are strictly forbidden.

Originally, the "zone" was not considered a diet, but an eating lifestyle. While that continues to be true, by popular demand it has evolved into a diet as well. Meal plans are available on Dr. Sears' web site: www.zonediet.com.

People who live in "the zone" usually experience some weight loss, but more importantly, notice an improvement in the lean body mass to fatty tissue ratio. (They look more slim and trim.) Those suffering from chronic inflammation such as headaches and arthritis also report noticeable improvement when on the plan. Others who have been suffering the effects of low blood sugar report higher energy levels and improved ability to stay focused on tasks. Entering "the zone" is a good way to increase your effectiveness.

THE SOUTH BEACH DIET

Dr. Arthur Agaston, M.D. is a cardiologist who practices in Miami, Florida's South Beach. He utilized some of the latest research findings in nutrition to devise a safe, healthy diet for his overweight heart patients. When the news media in Miami did stories on his new diet, it became a sensation in the Miami area. Eventually the story spread nation-wide. Now he has written the New York Times best-selling book, *The South Beach Diet: The Delicious, Doctor-Designed, Foolproof Plan for Fast and Healthy Weight Loss*. He also has a web site, www.southbeachdiet.com, offering a free newsletter and a paid subscription to a weekly meal planning service.

His approach is similar to Dr. Barry Sears' "zone," since it pays special attention to the glycemic index factor of food. It also incorporates the phased approach used successfully by the Atkins diet. Each of the three phases lasts for two weeks and then continues in two-week cycles. Phase one is rather strict, eliminating all bread and fruit, for example. Each successive phase re-introduces foods to the diet until you are eating just about every kind of food again, except for things like refined sugar. Since the meals are planned for you, you do not have to count calories or even "eyeball" portion sizes, as in the "zone."

Weight loss is a secondary goal of the diet. Its primary objective is to improve the chemistry of your blood to promote a healthy cardio-vascular system. It seems to accomplish both goals.

The ratio of carbohydrates, protein and fats, although not stated explicitly in the book, appears to be slightly different from the "zone." The ratio of carbohydrates seems to be slightly higher, protein slightly lower, and fats significantly lower—particularly saturated fats—than in the "zone."

There are a few nutritional and health concerns about the diet. One is the use of artificial sweeteners. Most artificial sugar substitutes—with the possible exception of saccharine—either have posed negative health risks or have not been in use long enough to prove that they are safe. Another concern is the use of egg whites without the yolks. Some nutritionists think that the body can better utilize eggs when they are consumed whole. Removing the yolks creates a nutritional imbalance. The same principle applies to the use of low-fat milk and dairy products advocated by the diet.

THE "CURVES" PROGRAM

Gary Heavin is the founder of Curves International, the largest fitness franchise in the world. Dedicated to helping women achieve fitness, he has devised a multi-faceted diet/exercise program that utilizes the latest research on diet and nutrition combined with his own approach based on over twenty-five years of experience as a health and nutrition counselor.

The Curves program incorporates some of the advances used by other diets, but seeks to avoid their pitfalls. Like the Atkins and South Beach diets, Curves uses a phased approach. The first phase is stringent, designed for relatively rapid weight loss. The second phase is less stringent and maintains gradual weight loss until you attain your desired weight. The third phase is lenient, allowing for "normal" sensible eating most of the time and dieting for only two days a month, in most cases, to keep weight in check.

The key to effectiveness for the Curves program is its metabolic adjustment technique. The problem inherent in most diets is your body's natural response to a reduction in food consumption. As soon as you begin to eat less food, your body reduces the rate at which it burns food, becoming more efficient. That is why weight loss rates usually level out shortly after any diet begins, and also why you gain most of the weight back, and more, if you discontinue the diet. The Curves diet surmounts this hurdle by limiting the time you are on the restricted regimen and actually increasing the amount of food consumed when weight loss plateaus. This approach, combined with resistance exercise three days per week, keeps the body in a fat-burning mode.

Another advantage to the Curves program is its flexibility. There are two tracks the dieter can follow, determined by her individual body chemistry and current needs. One track is designed for women who are sensitive to carbohydrates. It focuses on reducing carbohydrate consumption.

For women who are genetically blessed and have little or no sensitivity to carbohydrates, track two focuses on calorie reduction. Calorie counting can be tedious and difficult, but the Curves program offers help. Tasty recipes and meal plans are provided with the calories counted for you. Calorie counting guides are suggested for eating away from home during phase one. Watching calories when you eat in a restaurant is easier now, since an increasing number of chains are including carb and calorie counts for some of the items on their menus. Otherwise, some simple guidelines see you safely through the dieting minefields of restaurants and fast food outlets.

The best way the diet helps is to limit the time you are on a strict calorie counting regimen. In the third stage, you may not need to count calories for more than two days per month. The rest of the time, you follow the general pattern of a 2,500 to 3,000 calories-per-day diet, which is within the comfort range for most women. The program gives you practical guidelines for gauging portion size without weighing or measuring.

Another difficulty with calorie counting is getting up from the table before your appetite is satisfied. The Curves program offers a list of "free" foods that can be consumed without counting their calories. They are, for the most part, high-fiber complex carbohydrates, but also include a high-protein shake. That way, you can enjoy the feeling of being full after meals and avoid cravings between meals.

A rapidly growing number of women are proving that the Curves program works. It balances healthy eating and exercise. Although the fitness centers offer expert trainers, support and convenience, the program can be fully implemented at home with minimal, inexpensive equipment.

FRENCH LESSONS

Many Americans have grown weary going from one diet to another, because dieting is difficult any way you do it. No wonder they are eagerly turning to a different approach. Mirelle Guiliano offers it in her book, *French Women Don't Get Fat.* Although the French rarely diet, only 10 percent of adults are clinically obese, compared to 30 per cent of Americans. What is the difference? It is habits and attitudes based on the culture.

The French take more time to enjoy their meals. They like to sit leisurely with friends and family at a table set with pretty china. Even in fast food restaurants, the French stay longer than Americans. For example, McDonald's has observed that the average sit down time in their French outlets is 22.2 minutes, compared to 14.4 in the U.S.[16] Your body has what is popularly called an "appestat." It is the feeling of fullness when you have eaten a sufficient quantity of food at a meal. If you eat too fast, you consume more food than your body needs before the appestat has time to take effect.

The French eat rich, gourmet foods, but they habitually eat smaller portions. Paul Rozin, a psychologist at the University of Pennsylvania, and Claude Fischler, a French sociologist, made a study comparing French and American cultures. One of their findings was that Americans generally eat 25 per cent larger portions of comparable meals. The French frequently leave food on their plates, but Americans usually eat the entire serving, probably out of habit rather than hunger. They also noted a difference in attitude toward food. When they asked Americans to react to the words, "chocolate cake," they said, "Guilt." The French responded, "Celebration."[17] That is reminiscent of the apostle, Paul's, words, "Blessed is the man who does not condemn himself by what he approves." (Romans 14:22) Another way the French compensate for eating rich food is to balance one meal with another. If they eat a big lunch, they will offset it with a light soup supper.

The French way of eating is essentially using common sense. By slowing down to eat, they give their bodies a chance to regulate food consumption naturally. They enjoy real, wholesome food in moderation. Americans, on the other hand, often compulsively consume sweetened or salted processed foods because their taste buds are artificially over-stimulated.[18]

HOW SHOULD WE THEN EAT?

Here are a few common-sense suggestions that come out of the information you have just read. For more detailed guidance, see the Appendix, which lists resources for further study.

First, try to avoid the foods that contain harmful substances. Read product labels and choose foods with the least additives. Be especially watchful for hydrogenated vegetable fats and trans-fatty acids. Avoid most commercially fried and baked food. If you must eat fried food, cook it at home with fresh oil, such as peanut or canola. The healthiest oil that is readily available is extra virgin olive oil. Use it for sautéing meats and vegetables. However, always use low to medium heat settings. If the oil smokes, it is too hot, and is breaking down into harmful substances. When eating in restaurants, choose grilled or baked entrees over fried.

Familiarize yourself with the glycemic index. Note the foods you eat most often, and decide on what is a safe portion size. Do not eat high glycemic foods by themselves as a snack, such as carrots or bagels. Always eat them with protein and fats.

Eat mostly whole foods. Avoid refined white flour and sugar. If you want to eat pasta, choose those made from whole grains, and limit portion size; likewise for bread and bagels.

Be wary of any diet plan or food characterized by the words "high" or "low." With few exceptions, they are probably out of balance, and will not contribute to optimum nutritional benefits.

When planning your meals or ordering in a restaurant, here are some simple memory clues to help you make wise choices:

1. *Eat like a child.* Children instinctively know how to eat in a healthy way; but their sophisticated parents discourage them from following it early in life. For example, children prefer to eat one kind of food at a time. It is best to start with your meat, then eat your vegetables, and finish with fruits and sweets. That way, the protein and fats slow the absorption of sugars into the bloodstream and help to avoid an insulin response. By the way, children also like to eat their bread without the crust. That is a good idea, because the crust of the bread has been subjected to high baking temperatures that break fats down into harmful substances. The inside of the loaf never rises above 212 degrees, the boiling point of water.

2. *Eat like a bird.* We are not suggesting that you go hungry. Contrary to popular opinion, birds are voracious eaters. A barn swallow will consume one and one-half times its body weight in insects in a day. We do not recommend that you eat that much! Birds eat continually throughout the day, and they eat small portions. Plan to eat a healthy snack between meals so that you do not go much over four hours without eating something. That will keep your blood sugar from dipping too low between meals or spiking too high when you eat a meal that is too big. You will sleep better if you eat a balanced bedtime snack.

3. *Eat like a rabbit.* Rabbits love to eat vegetables, especially green leafy ones. Also, you never see a rabbit stirring a steaming saucepan. They eat their veggies raw, and so should you. That way, you get all the vitamins, enzymes and other phyto-nutrients that are usually lost in the cooking process. A good rule of thumb is to eat 40% of your vegetables raw in salads, dishes like stuffed tomatoes, or just plain. Use lemon juice and extra virgin olive oil for a dressing on your salads. Olive oil is also excellent seasoning for cooked vegetables. It is a good source of healthy fat and helps to tone down high glycemic foods; so it is a good addition to almost every meal.

4. *Eat like a monkey.* Monkeys love fruits. Make them your dessert of choice most of the time. Fruit sugar (fructose) is slow to digest, so it is less likely to provoke an insulin response than the refined sugar in cakes, cookies and other sweets. Fruits are also good for snacks if you combine them with other food containing protein and fat. They are loaded with nutrients, so you are not consuming "empty" calories when you eat them. Blueberries are especially nutritious as well as most other berries. Go light on banana, pineapple, watermelon or mango because of their high glycemic index.

5. *Eat like a squirrel.* Squirrels like to eat nuts. They are a great combination of protein and healthy fats. Choose raw over toasted, and avoid honey or sugar coatings. Be sure to include nuts in your snacks, especially almonds, macadamias and hazelnuts, but do not eat more than four to six of them at one time. Walnuts are an excellent choice because they do not contain as much fat as most other nuts. You can afford to eat more of them to satisfy your hunger than you could almonds, for example.

6. *Eat like a cat.* Cats prefer to eat fish and birds. There is an ugly rumor that they like to eat mice (red meat) but it is simply not true. They only eat mice when they cannot find any-

thing better to eat. Fish do not contain the saturated fats that are in red meats. Cold-water marine fish like salmon and tuna are good sources of omega-3 essential fatty acids. The best salmon are "wild" from the northern Pacific. Wild salmon feed on krill and other tiny marine animals that are rich in natural nutrients. Farm-raised Atlantic salmon are limited in their diets to commercial fish food. Chicken and turkey white meats are also lower in saturated fats than beef, pork or lamb, yet they are excellent sources of protein. It is not harmful for most people to enjoy eating red meats occasionally. They are an excellent source of B-vitamins; and a moderate amount of saturated fats in the diet is good for you.

7. *Eat like a mouse.* Mice like to eat cheese. Good sources of protein, calcium and vitamin D, dairy products have a place in a healthy diet; but because they contain sugar (lactose) and fats (saturated fats and arachidonic fatty acid) their consumption should be carefully limited. Generally, the soft cheeses like feta or Parmesan are better for you than the hard cheeses like cheddar or Swiss because of the calorie content. Sprinkle them over your salads for extra flavor and nutrition. Milk is easier to digest if you eat it in the form of yogurt (plain, not sweetened or combined with fruit unless it is fresh fruit that you add yourself).[19]

Hopefully you are ready to break that downward spiral that results from poor nutrition. When you begin to eat a balanced diet, you will find it much easier to bring the rest of your life into balance. Once you master the principles of healthy eating, it will not take much more time than you were spending on food anyway. The benefits will actually free up more usable time as you become healthier, more energetic and focused.

CHAPTER 9

Your Body:
Is It a Fit Place to Live?

EXERCISE AND BUSY-NESS

If you are too busy to exercise, you are too busy to live. Insufficient exercise results in declining strength, stamina, mental acuity and ability to focus. If you are already having difficulty keeping up with the demands of your busy schedule, then the lack of exercise will make maintaining your present pace increasingly difficult.

On the other hand, when you exercise regularly, the opposite occurs. You experience an increase in strength and stamina, or at least have little difficulty maintaining sufficient levels for all your activities. Your mental acuity remains sharp and your ability to stay focused on tasks will be strong. Exercise helps you to relax during the day and to sleep better at night, so that you feel refreshed and energized every morning. When you exercise, you are less likely to worry and be worn down emotionally by anxiety.

Exercise is one of the best stress relievers. An active lifestyle, even if not compulsively busy, will produce enough stress to become harmful if not relieved regularly. Exercise actually facilitates the dissipation of adrenaline in the blood and stimulates secretion of endorphins, resulting in a sense of euphoria that has sometimes been labeled a "runner's high."

Besides programming too many different things into every day's schedule, another reason you are neglecting some of the most important things in life could be lack of sufficient energy. You may be spending too much time on essential tasks because you do not have the energy to do them quickly and efficiently. If your mind is clouded, you will spend time correcting mistakes that could have been avoided if your mind were sharp. Regular exercise might actually add more usable time to your busy schedule than the twenty or thirty minutes per day it requires.

MAKE IT FUN.

Establishing and maintaining a consistent habit of exercise requires determination and discipline, but they may not be enough by themselves. You are more likely to succeed and continue to exercise if it involves activities you enjoy. If you like sports activities, then basketball, soccer or racquetball would be good choices. Otherwise, walking or jogging might work for you. If you get bored with going around the same track or neighborhood, then bicycling might have more appeal. If you live in a hot climate, then swimming is an inviting option. When exercise becomes drudgery, you will find excuses to give it up. Choose activities that you will look forward to doing, and you will stick with them.

SUIT YOUR PERSONALITY.

Consider who you are when choosing ways to exercise. For example, being around other people energizes extrovert personalities, but it drains energy from introverts. If you are an extrovert, choose sports that require a teammate, or find a "buddy" to share your walks or bike rides. Introverts will enjoy doing most of their exercise alone.

Use the right combination.

There are three components to a balanced exercise plan:

1. Aerobics: promoting adequate blood circulation and oxygenation
2. Resistance: developing muscle tone and strength
3. Flexibility: maintaining range of motion

It is not necessary to join a health club or buy expensive equipment to begin an exercise program. A few simple activities you can do at home or at the office will put you in good shape, as long as they include the three necessary components.

Aerobic exercises

Any exercise that utilizes groups of large muscles continuously for a sustained period of time is considered aerobic. The primary purpose is to elevate your heart rate for the duration of the exercise period and strengthen the cardiovascular system. Other benefits include increased stamina and excess fat reduction.

Activities such as jogging, brisk walking, hiking, cycling, skating, swimming, cross-country skiing, rowing, racquetball, dance/group exercises, and jumping rope qualify as aerobic exercise. For consistency, it is helpful to have some provision for exercising indoors when the weather outside is not suitable. A treadmill is a good example, but less expensive devices work as well. The mini-trampoline gives an excellent workout and is much easier on your joints than a treadmill or other machines. The newer models have a balance bar for better stability and safety. High intensity aerobic exercise should be curtailed or avoided outdoors when the weather is extremely hot and humid, unless it is swimming. If you must exercise outdoors in a hot climate, do it early in the morning or late afternoon when temperatures are moderate.

Whatever activity you choose, be sure to include warm-up and cool-down periods. They only need to last three to five minutes. The simplest way is to perform the same exercise at a low level of intensity. So, if you are walking start at a leisurely pace and then speed up after your muscles get warm. Likewise, go back to the leisurely pace for a few minutes to let the muscles cool down before you end the exercise session.

There are three things to consider when planning aerobic exercise:

* *Frequency*
  The general rule is three to five days per week. If general fitness is your goal, then three days could be enough. If your goal is to lose a little weight, then five days would be more beneficial.

* *Intensity*
  This will vary for each individual. Of course, if you are not accustomed to exercise, then start at a low intensity and gradually work your way up to higher levels. Actually, it is not necessary to attain high levels of intensity to improve your health significantly. For example, brisk walking is as beneficial for most people as jogging. High levels of intensity are difficult to sustain, and could discourage you from continuing your exercise program. Also, the risk of injuries is greater at higher levels.

  Although there are formulas for measuring intensity using your pulse rate, a simple guideline will suffice for most people. It is the "talk test." If you can carry on a conversation while exercising, then the intensity level is not too high. On the other hand, if your breathing becomes so labored that you cannot speak coherently, then your exercise is too intense and if a high level is maintained for an extended time, you may be endangering your health.

* *Duration*
  Again, depending on the intensity of the exercise, there is no hard and fast rule. Twenty to sixty minutes per day is the recommended duration. Also, you do not have to do the exercise all at one time. For example, three ten-minute sessions

can be as beneficial as one thirty-minute session. The variable is the level of intensity. You need to walk for at least thirty minutes, for instance, to benefit significantly; but you could achieve a beneficial result in twenty minutes jumping rope. (For more information see Edward Jackowski's book, *Escape Your Shape.*)

RESISTANCE EXERCISES

Resistance training will complete your fitness program. Not only does it strengthen your muscles, it also increases mineral density in your bones and improves the ratio of fat to body mass. Unfortunately, there are hardly any sports or fun activities that systematically perform strength training for your various muscle groups except weight lifting. If you enjoy health clubs or can afford to set up a little gym in your home, that is a fine way to do resistance training. On the other hand, you can do most of the training you need to do with a relatively inexpensive set of weights or "figure 8" elastic bands from a sporting goods store. You will need to study some of the basic principles of weight lifting to use them safely and effectively.

Abs

Start

Finish

3 sets, 12-15 reps per set

Abs - Elbow to Knee

Start

Finish

Alternate right and left elbow to knee

Back

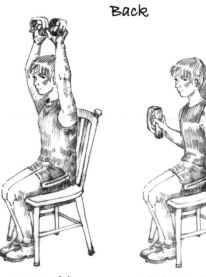

Start Position   Finish Position

3 sets - 12 to 15 reps per set

Bicep

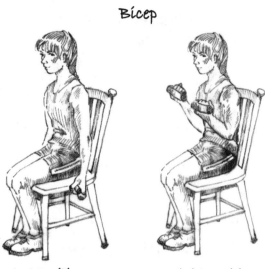

Start Position   **Finish Position**

3 sets - 12 to 15 reps per set

Calf Raises

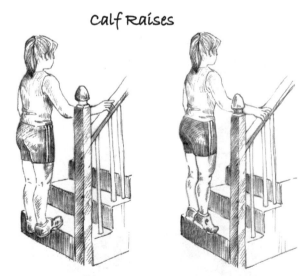

Start Position   **Finish Position**

3 sets - 12 to 15 reps per set

Chest Push-up

Start Position   Finish Position

3 sets - 8 to 10 reps per set

Squats

Start Position   Finished Position

3 sets, 12 to 15 reps per set

Tricep

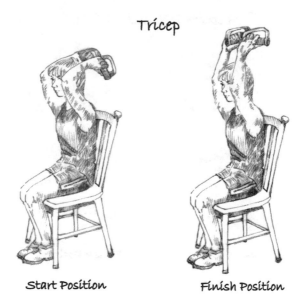

Start Position   Finish Position

3 sets - 12 to 15 reps per set

Figure 8 Band - Back

Start Position   Finish Position

3 sets - 12 to 15 reps per set

Figure 8 Band - Bicep

Start Position   Finish Position

3 sets - 12 to 15 reps per set

Figure 8 Band - Chest

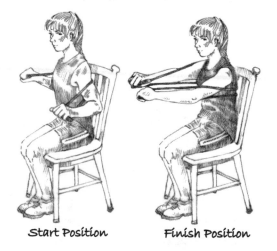

Start Position   Finish Position

3 sets - 12 to 15 reps per set

Figure 8 Band - Hamstring

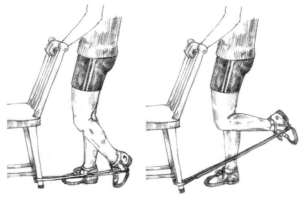

Start Position   Finish Position

3 sets - 12 to 15 reps per set

Figure 8 Band - Quad

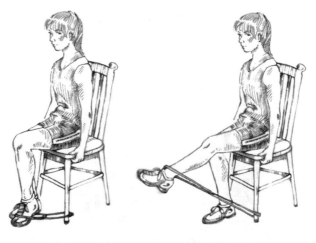

Start Position   Finish Position

3 sets - 12 to 15 reps per set

Figure 8 Band - Shoulder

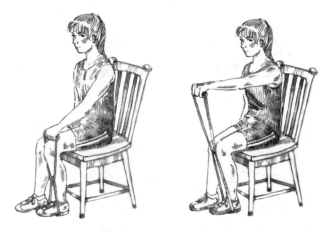

Start Position   Finish Position

3 sets - 12 to 15 reps per set

Figure 8 Band - Tricep

Start Position   Finish Position

3 sets - 12 to 15 reps per set

FLEXIBILITY EXERCISES

Concentrated stretching exercises should be done at least twice per week, but no more than five times. Light stretches can be beneficial every day. The key to good stretches is gentleness. Forget about "No pain, no gain." If you feel pain while you are stretching, you are doing too much too fast, and are liable to cause injury to muscles or ligaments.

Generally, it is best to do stretching exercises at the end of your workout. Muscles that have just been stretched are more likely to be injured during strenuous activity. Women are more susceptible than men to knee and ankle injuries resulting from too much stretching or stretching before athletic activity.[1]

Progressive muscular relaxation (PMR) is a technique that dramatically enhances stretching exercise. This technique was used in Russia before it began to catch on in America. Pavel Tsatsouline was a trainer for Special Forces in the Soviet Union. He warns that muscles should not be stretched until they are relaxed. When muscles become shorter and stiffen, he adds, it is not because of anything in the muscle tissue itself. It is a result of neurological impulses from the brain. If you force a muscle to stretch while it is still partially contracted, you will cause small tears. When they heal, scar tissue forms, and the muscle will be even less flexible. The best way to coax a muscle to relax is to contract it and hold the contraction until the muscle becomes fatigued. When you release the contraction, the brain sends a message to the muscle that it is OK to relax. Then the muscle will stretch without tearing.

Tsatsouline points out that your body naturally will not allow a range of motion that your muscles do not have sufficient strength to control. By combining isometric exercise with stretching, you are strengthening the muscles while you stretch them. Most traditional stretching exercises can be adapted to this combined approach. As a plus, you are saving time in your exercise program by accomplishing two of the essential components simultaneously.

The authors recommend a few examples of stretching exercises that can be done in the home or at the office:

1. Calf Muscle Leg Stretch
   - Stand about three or four feet from a wall, facing it squarely.
   - Keeping the right leg straight and your heel firmly on the floor, step forward with your left foot and lean onto the wall with both hands.
   - Keep both feet pointing straight towards the wall and parallel to each other.
   - Flex the muscle in your right leg and buttock and hold the contraction for several minutes until your calf begins to quiver and feel fatigued.
   - Release the tension and gently lean toward the wall, stretching the right calf.
   - Repeat the procedure with the left leg straight and the right leg bent.

2. Shoulder Stretch
   - With shoulders relaxed, raise your right arm parallel to the floor and swing it across your chest, keeping your elbow straight.
   - With your left arm, reach under your right arm and grasp it just above the elbow.
   - Push out with your right arm while resisting with your left arm and hold for several seconds to a minute.
   - Release the tension and gently press the right arm toward the chest with the left arm.
   - Repeat the procedure with the arms reversed.

3. Neck/Spine Stretch
   - While standing, or sitting in a chair, relax your shoulders and let your left arm hang by your side.
   - Reach over your head with your right arm and grasp your head behind your left ear. Lower your chin slightly toward your chest.
   - Gently push your head against your right hand while it resists, holding the tension for a few seconds to a minute.

- Release the tension and using only the weight of your hand, pull your head down toward your right shoulder.
- Repeat the procedure with the arm positions reversed.

4. Hamstring Stretch
   - Lie flat on your back on the floor, couch or bed.
   - Extend your right leg straight out in line with your body.
   - Raise your left thigh and hold it at about a 45-degree angle with both hands.
   - Tense the muscles in your thigh and buttocks, and hold for up to a minute.
   - Release the tension, then slowly and gently straighten your left knee until you feel the stretch. Hold the stretch for about ten seconds and release.
   - Repeat the procedure with the right leg.

For more detailed instruction about stretching exercises, consult the following resources:

Relax Into Stretch: Instant Flexibility Through Mastering Muscle Tension by Pavel Tsatsouline, ©2001, Dragon Door Publications, Inc. ISBN 0-938045-28-8 (Order online at www.dragondoor. com.)

Stretching in the Office by Bob Anderson, © 2002, Shelter Publications, ISBN 936070-29-3 (Order online at www.shelterpub. com.)

Stretching: 20th Anniversary Revised Edition by Bob Anderson, © 2000, Shelter Publications, ISBN 0-936070-22-6 (Order online at www.shelterpub.com.)

GET READY FOR A NEW YOU.
Once you begin to experience the benefits of regular exercise, you will wonder why you waited so long to begin. The first

thing you may notice is an energy level increase. You will become more effective at work, or be more able to keep up with your grandchildren. You can get more tasks done in less time, freeing up time for other priorities, such as time with your family or for solitude, silence and devotions.

Muscle tone will improve and your body will look more trim, even if you don't lose much weight. If you train for weight loss, you will notice results there, too, when your clothes don't fit as tightly as before.

Range of motion will increase. You won't feel as stiff, and you will be able to tie your shoelaces or reach under a kitchen counter without hurting. You will be free to take up a new hobby or sport, or be able to continue some of the ones you used to enjoy.

You will feel relief from much of the stress in your life. Sleep will come easier for you, and you will wake up more refreshed in the mornings, in less need of caffeine stimulants.

Perhaps most importantly, your heart and circulatory system will be healthier. You could be adding years to your life expectancy: more time to achieve your life's goals and to be with your loved ones.

The most difficult obstacle you will face in your exercise program is getting started. Begin, and the rest is easy.

CHAPTER 10

12 Steps to Recovery from Busy-ness Addiction

The bad news is that excessive busy-ness is an addiction. The good news is that there are tried and proven methods to recover from addictions. One of them is the "12 Steps to Recovery" used successfully by Alcoholics Anonymous. A comparison of the 12 steps with biblical principles for human behavior reveals not only compatibility, but also some correlation. A.A. utilizes the 12 steps in conjunction with group meetings, but an individual can use the principles effectively. The wording has been changed to apply to busy-ness addiction on an individual basis from a Christian viewpoint. Many of the ideas for adapting the 12 steps to busy-ness addiction were inspired by *Serenity: A Companion for 12 Step Recovery* by Robert Hemfelt and Richard Fowler (Thomas Nelson, Publishers, 1990).[1]

---

[1] We as authors realize many who read this book do not adhere to the Judeo-Christian worldview. Our request is that this approach be explored with an open mind.

Step 1. Admit that you are not able to deal with busy-ness addiction in your own strength—that your life is out of balance.

To admit that you lack the power to manage your life is difficult in a culture that idolizes being a "winner," and regards the humiliation of "losers" as entertainment. Yet, that is exactly what you must do to break the addictive cycle. All addictions are based on underlying assumptions such as, "The more you use, the better you will feel; you can stop any time you want; you can handle it."

Admission of defeat is the first step to victory and recovery, which is a paradox, like many that Jesus taught. It is by giving that you receive (Luke 6:38); it is by serving that you rise to spiritual leadership (Matthew 20:27); and it is by losing your life that you find it (Matthew 10:39). A paradox seems to be contradictory until it is considered in the context of a greater reality, a larger body of information. Then it begins to make sense. The necessity of admitting one's own powerlessness makes perfectly good sense when you understand the cycle of addiction. The addictive cycle goes through five stages:

1. **Pain**
    For busy-ness addiction, the pain usually is in the form of fear: of failure to achieve perfectionist goals, of humiliation, inadequacy, missing out on the good life, facing the banality and purposelessness of one's life, old age and ultimately death.

2. **The Addictive Agent**
    To alleviate his pain, the person fills his life with activities that make him feel like a "winner." He becomes a workaholic at his job. At church he might volunteer for responsibilities that require more time than his busy schedule reasonably allows. Even his play becomes highly competitive and stressful.

3. **Temporary Relief**
    Our culture rewards excessive busy-ness. His employer praises him for being a hard worker and holds him up as an

example to the other employees. He gets promotions and salary increases. His pastor and other church leaders, likewise, praise him for his tireless efforts to sustain and advance the church's programs. His prowess on the golf course assures him that he is, indeed, a "winner."

4. Negative Results

Unfortunately, the result is that he loses contact with his family and has no time for developing a spiritual relationship with God. Eventually, he may experience health problems varying from fatigue to a heart attack. Emotionally he may suffer from bouts of depression or struggle with uncontrolled anger.

5. Guilt Syndrome

When he realizes that he is failing in these areas, a guilt syndrome begins. He feels compelled to work harder than ever to assuage his guilt.

When a person is caught in a syndrome like this, the sensible thing to do is to break it and get out; but the addict does not do that for two reasons. One is the fear of withdrawal. Until recently, the common wisdom among doctors who treat drug and alcohol addictions was that withdrawal symptoms were mainly biochemical and physical. Now they realize that the main factors in withdrawal are spiritual and emotional. That is particularly true in the case of busy-ness addiction, since the addiction is not to a substance, but to a behavior. When a busy-ness addict tries to scale back his activities, the withdrawal pains stem from the person's fear that he is losing control; but his being in control is the source of his problem. He was in control when he chose to engage in the addictive behavior in the first place. He was in control when he convinced himself that he could handle the problem without outside help; and he remains in control when he refuses to take the necessary steps to break the addictive syndrome.

The other reason is denial, a self-deception that shields the person from an honest assessment of his problem. The person in denial tells himself, "When I decide to stop, I can do it. Things aren't as bad as they seem. I am behaving this way because it is what I want. If my situation changes for the better (or gets worse), then I will change my behavior." Sometimes the workaholic will project responsibility onto someone else. He thinks, "I have to work like this to support the lifestyle my family expects."

As a rule, most people caught in the cycle of an addiction will not admit that they lack the power to overcome their addiction until they reach a crisis point. It is often referred to as "hitting bottom." It occurs in one or more of the physical, emotional and spiritual areas of life. Frequently, it happens when the spouse asks for a divorce. A parent could realize that he or she has lost the relationship with a child. It could be the first heart attack, or chronic fatigue that interferes with one's ability to function. Less often, but most important, it could be a realization that one is spiritually bankrupt and alienated from God.

When one has hit bottom, then he may become willing to face the negative consequences of his addictive behavior. The workaholic, for example, needs to admit that his over-commitment in the areas of his career, volunteer work and compulsive recreation habits have caused him to deny his family the time necessary to cultivate intimate emotional relationships. Spiritually, it has caused him to neglect the disciplines of personal prayer and devotion, leaving him out of touch with God.

The apostle, Paul, admitted his powerlessness in Romans 7:15 and 18. "I do not understand what I do. For what I want to do I do not do, but what I hate I do…I know that nothing good lives in me, that is, in my sinful nature. For I have the desire to do what is good, but I cannot carry it out." That is how he broke through to victory over his besetting sins. In the final analysis, there is no other way.

The person caught in the busy-ness addiction syndrome is ready to experience victory when he admits that his own self-effort is insufficient to change his behavior. Then he can say with Paul, "...For when I am weak, then I am strong." (II Corinthians 12:10) When you stop relying on your own power, then you are ready to receive power from a source outside of yourself that will restore healthy balance to your life. That is the next step.

Step 2. Trust in the power of God's Holy Spirit to bring your life back into balance and wellness.

To trust in God's power is to rely confidently on it to meet your needs. This power is available to all who will abandon their own self-efforts and accept it on the terms God offers. When Zerubabel faced the seemingly impossible job of rebuilding the temple in Jerusalem after the Babylonian captivity, the prophet, Zechariah, delivered this message to him from God, "'Not by might nor by power, but by my Spirit,' says the Lord Almighty." (Zechariah 4:6) Zerubabel could not complete the task assigned to him in his own power, but with the power of God flowing through him, he accomplished his mission.

How do you receive power from God's Spirit? Jesus answered this question one night when a Jewish rabbi, Nicodemus, came to him for a consultation. Jesus confronted him with this startling statement: "I tell you the truth, no one can see the kingdom of God unless he is born again." (John 3:3) Nicodemus was confused, thinking Jesus was speaking literally. Jesus explained that he was referring to a spiritual birth. "I tell you the truth, no one can enter the kingdom of God unless he is born of water [physical birth] and the Spirit. Flesh gives birth to flesh, but the Spirit gives birth to spirit." (John 3:5-6) After a brief reference to His approaching death on the cross, Jesus gave Nicodemus this invitation, "For God so loved the world that he gave his one and only son, that whoever believes in him shall not perish but have eternal life." (John 3:16)

The apostle, Paul, explained how Christ's death did for us what we could not do for ourselves. "You see, at just the right time, when we were still powerless, Christ died for the ungodly." (Romans 5:6) The apostle, John, clarifies the significance of Christ's death. "This is love: not that we loved God, but that he loved us and sent his Son as an atoning sacrifice for our sins." (I John 4:10) That means that Jesus Christ paid the penalty that we deserved for our sins to satisfy God's cosmic standard of justice. He could do that because He had no sins of his own to die for. When He died as our sinless substitute, He earned infinite merit for us in God's system of justice. Paul stated this fact in II Corinthians 5:21, "God made him who had no sin to be sin for us, so that in him we might become the righteousness of God." In another reference to Christ's death as an atoning sacrifice, Paul wrote, "...[God] did it to demonstrate his justice at the present time, so as to be just and the one who justifies those who have faith in Jesus." (Romans 3: 26)

This is the gospel message—the "good news." It means that sinful human beings can be dramatically changed. We can be rescued from bondage to sin, death and eternal punishment for our sins. It also means we can recover from addictions that are degrading the quality of our lives. We can receive a new quality of life—eternal life—the kind of life that God possesses in Himself. It begins the moment you trust in the death and resurrection of Jesus Christ as the basis for forgiveness of your sins. It continues for eternity. Jesus told Martha at the tomb of Lazarus, "I am the resurrection and the life. He who believes in me will live, even though he dies; and whoever lives and believes in me will never die." (John 11:25) Jesus demonstrated the truth of this statement by rising from the dead three days after His crucifixion. When Mary Magdalene and another woman named Mary went to the tomb where Jesus' body had been laid to rest they encountered an angel who said, "...Do not be afraid, for I know that you are looking for Jesus, who was crucified. He is not here; he has risen, just as he said..." (Matthew 28:5-6)

How much power did it take to raise Jesus from the dead? Astronautic engineers can design rocket engines powerful enough to propel a manned space ship to the nearest planet, Mars, but there is no human power on Earth that can raise a man from the dead. Yet that is the power that Christ gives to anyone who trusts in Him for salvation. "But, because of his great love for us, God, who is rich in mercy, made us alive with

Christ even when we were dead in transgressions—it is by grace you have been saved. And God raised us up with Christ and seated us with him in the heavenly realms in Christ Jesus, in order that in the coming ages he might show the incomparable riches of his grace, expressed in his kindness to us in Christ Jesus." (Ephesians 2: 4-7)

The power that Christ imparts to the believer is the power that created the universe. The Gospel of John states that Christ as the eternal Word was the agent of creation. "In the beginning was the Word, and the Word was with God, and the Word was God. He was with God in the beginning. Through him all things were made; without him nothing was made that has been made." (John 1:1-3) Paul describes how that power impacts the life of one who has received salvation through faith in Christ. "Therefore, if anyone is in Christ, he is a new creation; the old has gone, the new has come!" (II Corinthians 5:17) You may feel that your case is hopeless; that you have gone too far into your problems ever to return to balance and wellness. But no one is beyond God's power to reclaim and restore unless they choose to be. The decision is up to you.

Step 3. Decide to yield your will and your life to God's control.

To receive this power from God, you must change your mind about some crucial issues. The Bible refers to this experience as "repentance." When the apostle, Paul, was bidding farewell to the church he established at Ephesus, he noted that repentance was an integral part of the message he preached. "I have declared to both Jews and Greeks that they must turn to God in repentance and have faith in our Lord Jesus." (Acts 20:21)

What are these issues that you must change your mind about? Some of them are general and apply to everyone; and some of them may be specific and apply to each individual differently. Generally, you must change your mind about who Jesus is. If you have been thinking that Jesus was a legendary figure, just another great teacher, or one of many martyrs who died for his ideals, you need to acknowledge Him as the divine Son of

God. Eventually, every creature in the universe will make this acknowledgment. "Who [Christ Jesus], being in very nature God, did not consider equality with God something to be grasped, but made himself nothing, taking the very nature of a servant, being made in human likeness. And being found in appearance as a man, he humbled himself and became obedient to death—even death on a cross! Therefore God exalted him to the highest place and gave him the name that is above every name, that at the name of Jesus every knee should bow, in heaven and on earth and under the earth, and every tongue confess that Jesus Christ is Lord, to the glory of God the Father." (Philippians 2:6-11) When you confess that Jesus is lord, you are yielding your will to His control, giving Him permission to guide and direct your life.

Next, you must change your mind about yourself. The first step is to recognize that you do not have the power or ability to perform up to God's standards. "But now a righteousness from God, apart from law, has been made known…This righteousness from God comes through faith in Jesus Christ to all who believe. There is no difference, for all have sinned and fall short of the glory of God, and are justified freely by His grace." (Romans 3:21-24)

After abandoning all hope of pleasing God by your own efforts, the next step is to trust in Christ's work on the cross for you and nothing else. "…If you confess with your mouth, 'Jesus is Lord,' and believe in your heart that God raised him from the dead, you will be saved. For it is with your heart that you believe and are justified, and it is with your mouth that you confess and are saved." (Romans 10:9-10) "For it is by grace you have been saved, through faith—and this not from yourselves, it is the gift of God—not by works, so that no one can boast." (Ephesians 2:8-9)

Specifically, you may need to examine your life and determine what you have trusted instead of coming to Christ with your need. It could be money, sex, power, success in your career, control of your life and abusive control of your family members' lives. Perhaps you have been playing god, focusing all of your attention on yourself and expecting everyone around you to do the same. You may have been relying on excessive busy-ness to give your life meaning and to avoid facing your spiritual need for forgiveness. Focusing on your self and your own needs and efforts tends to increase your pain, loneliness and isolation, drawing you deeper into your addiction. To break the pain cycle, you must turn to a source outside yourself and your own selfish pursuits.

Decide that you will no longer trust in anything other than your relationship with Christ to give you meaning, purpose and security in this life and the next. Ask Christ to give you the power to serve Him faithfully and live a life that is pleasing to Him. When you make that decision, your new life in Christ begins. Jesus promised that those who follow Him in discipleship will experience a superior quality of life. Comparing Himself to a shepherd who prepares a safe and secure enclosure for his sheep, Jesus said, "I am the gate; whoever enters through me will be saved. He will come in and go out, and find pasture. The thief comes only to steal and kill and destroy; I have come that they may have life, and have it to the full." (John 10:9-10)

Though you are secure in Christ, that does not mean there will be no struggles. Living the Christian life requires daily decisions to trust Christ in your circumstances, which can be difficult. "So then, just as you received Christ Jesus as Lord, continue to live in him, rooted and built up in him, strengthened in the faith as you were taught, and overflowing with thankfulness." (Colossians 2:6-7) As you struggle with your addiction to excessive busy-ness and attempt to scale back your commitments, you will repeatedly go through the process of admitting your powerlessness and trusting Christ for the power to make the changes needed in your lifestyle to restore balance and wellness. Then you can say with the apostle, Paul, "...I have learned the secret of being content in any and every situation, whether well fed or hungry, whether living in plenty or want. I can do everything through him who gives me strength." (Philippians 4:12-13)

Now that God's Spirit is empowering your life, you are ready to begin making the changes in your behavior to conform to His will. That is the next step.

Step 4. Take a complete moral inventory of your life and behavior.

This is not a task to take on by yourself. You need guidance. In His earthly ministry, Jesus led the Samaritan woman at the well to face up to her moral failures. He asked her to call her husband. When she replied that she did not have a husband, Jesus informed her that she had lived with five "husbands," and that the man she was living with was not her husband. (See John 4:16-18.) To write a journal of your life's story and face up to your failures can be a healthy, cleansing experience.

The apostle, Paul, assures us that the Holy Spirit will aid us when we take stock of our lives. Looking forward to the time when all of creation and our individual lives will be restored to perfect harmony with God, Paul recognized that believers have a long way to go and must wait patiently for their salvation to be complete. In the meantime, our responsibility is to pray that God will guide us a step at a time into His will for our lives. "In the same way, the Spirit helps us in our weakness. We do not know what we ought to pray for, but the Spirit himself intercedes for us with groans that words cannot express. And he who searches our hearts knows the mind of the Spirit, because the Spirit intercedes for the saints in accordance with God's will." (Romans 8:26-27) This is Spirit-guided prayer.

Our problem is ignorance. We do not know what we should pray for. That is, we do not know what God's priority is for bringing our lives into conformity with His will. It would be overwhelming if He were to deal with all our faults at once. Rather, He tends to single out one or two of our most important or urgent spiritual needs and bring them to our minds. Ask God to search your heart as you make your inventory. Write down every moral failure as it comes to mind. Then pray that God will show you which ones to address first.

As you review the relationships in your life, the logical starting point is your parents. It is fashionable in this perfectionist culture to blame your parents for not providing you with the perfect childhood—whatever that is. The fact is, they are fallible human beings that were struggling with some of the issues handed down to them from their parents while trying to provide a living and a better life for their children than they had. They were not perfect. They made mistakes.

For example, if your father was frustrated in his career and considered himself unsuccessful, he may have put undue pressure on his son or daughter to achieve. The impact on your life could be the perfectionist, compulsive tendencies that make you susceptible to busy-ness addiction. In turn, you could resent your father for being overbearing, hard driving and insensitive to your need for acceptance and affirmation.

Now that you are a father or mother, you probably have a tendency to treat your children the way your father treated you, and you are hurting them the same way your father hurt you. You cannot change your father's attitude. He may not even be alive any more. You cannot undo the past. What you can do is face up to your feelings of resentment toward your father and the negative tendencies he passed on to you and include them in your moral inventory so that you can do something about them. Continue this process with your other relationships, such as teachers, mentors, employers and supervisors, romantic interests or your spouse and children.

As you take your inventory, it is important to distinguish between true and false guilt. Sometimes we take the blame for the behavior of others over which we had no control. Children of parents with addictions, for instance, often become co-dependent and assume the role of parenting their parent. Then they feel responsible or ashamed for their parent's failure. This is false guilt.

If you are honest, you will find plenty of moral failures for which you are legitimately responsible. This is authentic guilt. Since we are basically selfish by nature, we say and do things that hurt or offend other people in the process of getting what we want in life or avoiding what we do not want. We neglect responsibilities to our parents, children, fellow Christians in the church, and others.

Your addiction to busy-ness is no doubt causing pain and hurt to members of your family. The long hours at work cause you to be an absentee parent. You were not there for the championship soccer game that your son or daughter played in. You worked late the night your daughter gave her first dance performance or music recital. They said they understood why you couldn't be there, but they got the message that your career (or golf game, or even volunteer work at the church) is more important to you than they are. That hurts.

You used to have a close, romantic relationship with your wife or husband. Now it is more a relationship of convenience. There never seems to be a good time for an intimate talk or a romantic dinner or other adventure that you share. The passion is gone. You have become like a stranger to your husband or wife. That hurts.

As you compile the inventory, do not anticipate how you will deal with all of the issues. That could be discouraging and bog you down as you uncover the issues that need to be addressed. Just list them objectively and dispassionately. The remaining steps will guide you through the process of dealing with your failures.

Step 5. Confess to God, yourself and one other person the specific things you have done wrong.

God has revealed His moral will in the Bible. It is summarized in the Ten Commandments (Exodus 20:1-17). Jesus elevated the standard and revealed its ultimate fulfillment in the Sermon on the Mount. (See Matthew, chapters 5-7.) It includes obligations and prohibitions. Confession is simply agreeing with God that your actions do not conform to His moral standards. The apostle, John, emphasized the necessity of confession. "If we claim to be without sin, we deceive ourselves and the truth is not in us. If we confess our sins, he is faithful and just and will forgive us our sins and purify us from all unrighteousness. If we claim we have not sinned, we make him out to be a liar and his word has no place in our lives." (I John 1:8-10)

Unconfessed sin erects a barrier between you and God. The prophet, Isaiah, wrote, "But your iniquities have separated you from your God; your sins have hidden his face from you, so that he will not hear." (Isaiah 59:2) It is pointless to try to conceal or deny our guilt before God, because He already knows about it. "For the word of God is living and active. Sharper than any double-edged sword, it penetrates even to dividing soul and spirit, joints and marrow; it judges the thoughts and attitudes of the heart. Nothing in all creation is hidden from God's sight. Everything is uncovered and laid bare before the eyes of him to whom we must give account." (Hebrews 4:12-13)

Confession to God forces you to break your pattern of denial and honestly face up to the true-guilt issues in your life. Then you are in a position to receive God's mercy and forgiveness. That was King David's experience. "When I kept silent, my bones wasted away through my groaning all day long. For day and night your hand was heavy upon me; my strength was sapped as in the heat of summer. Then I acknowledged my sin to you and did not cover up my iniquity. I said, 'I will confess my transgressions to the Lord' —and you forgave the guilt of my sin." (Psalm 32:3-5)

Confession is by nature a cleansing exercise that restores emotional health and balance. Receiving God's forgiveness frees you from your guilt and shame. Expressing the hurts, resentments, fears and anger you have felt in yourself and caused in others takes you through the grief process and brings relief. Breaking down the barrier between you and God draws you out of the isolation that characterizes addictions.

After becoming honest with yourself and God, you need to take one other person into your confidence. This action will draw you further out of your isolation. Be careful whom you select. In most cases, the best choice would probably not be your spouse or a close family member. Rather, choose someone trustworthy, who is objective, not involved in your personal relationships. Your pastor, a respected leader in your church, or a professional Christian counselor would be good choices. His affirmation and understanding can give you the confidence to confess to other people. Before you do that, there are a couple more steps to take in your relationship to God.

Step 6. Give God permission to remove the thought patterns and behaviors that contribute to busy-ness addiction.

God is a "gentleman." He does not force His will on you, but waits to act in your life until you give Him permission. You must be willing for changes to be made before you can expect God to help you. You also must be willing to make some changes that you did not anticipate as God brings them to your mind.

Jesus dealt with the necessity of willingness when He healed a man in Jerusalem at the pool called Bethesda. Periodically, the water in the pool would become roiled. It was believed that the first person to plunge into the pool after the water stirred would be healed of any affliction. Five porches surrounded this pool. Many disabled people lay in the shade of the porches, each one hoping to be the first to enter the water at the opportune moment. Jesus approached one of them, a man who had been lame for 38 years, and asked a peculiar question, "Do you want to get well?" (John 5:6) The man offered the excuse that he had no friend to help him into the water, so someone else always pushed ahead of him. Perhaps Jesus understood that the man's life would change dramatically if he were healed. For 38 years he had become accustomed to lying in the cool shade of the porch by the pleasant pool while able-bodied men went out into the fields to work all day in the hot sun. People felt sorry for him and gave him food to eat. He was a victim of his circumstances. He had no responsibilities and no expectations to meet. He could have become complacent in his situation; but when Jesus offered him a better way to live he willingly accepted it. "Then Jesus said to him, 'Get up! Pick up your mat and walk.' At once the man was cured; he picked up his mat and walked." (John 5:8) Jesus was willing from the start to help the man. The only question that needed to be settled was the man's own willingness to accept and embrace the changes that would occur in his life if Jesus helped him.

Are you truly willing to accept the changes in your lifestyle that will occur if you become free of busy-ness addiction? You may be willing to cut back on your demanding work schedule; but are you willing to give up a few rounds of golf or racquetball to free up more time to spend with your family? You may be willing to scale back the overcommitment to your church's programs and accept a less prominent role; but are you willing to spend more time in prayer, meditation in the Word, silence and solitude? These are some of the issues that need to be settled in your mind and heart.

Be careful not to go from one extreme to another. It is not good to be a workaholic and neglect your relationships to family, church and God. On the other hand, it is good to be diligent and industrious. The apostle, Paul, wrote to some Christians who had quit their jobs to wait for the rapture of the church. "We hear that some among you are idle. They are not busy; they are busybodies. Such people we command and urge in the Lord Jesus Christ to settle down and earn the bread they eat." (II Thessalonians 3:11-12) The important thing is for you to be willing for God to bring your life back into balance, whatever that may require.

Step 7. In faith and humility, ask God to remove the attitudes and desires that cause you to be addicted to busy-ness.

After establishing your willingness to be changed, the next step is to express your faith in God's willingness and ability to change you. That requires a spirit of humility. While you were caught in the addiction syndrome, you were placing your own desires and attitudes ahead of God's will for your life. To break the addiction, you must stop your rebellion and humbly submit to God's will.

You need not fear that God will take your submission as an opportunity to humiliate you. That is not His intention. Even though He almost certainly will lead you into some rigorous and difficult experiences, they will be designed to make you a better person and give meaning and purpose to your life. "Moreover, we have all had human fathers who disciplined us and we respected them for it. How much more should we submit to the Father of our spirits and live! Our fathers disciplined us for a little while as they thought best; but God disciplines us for our good, that we may share in his holiness. No discipline seems pleasant at the time, but painful. Later on, however, it produces a harvest of righteousness and peace for those who have been trained by it." (Hebrews 12:9-11)

Humbly submitting to God will not damage your self-esteem or create a bad self-image. Just the opposite is true. In your rebellion, you probably compensated for your feelings of insecurity and inadequacy by putting up a front, pretending to be more confident than you actually were. When you admit your inability to change and improve your life, you do not have to pretend any more. The moment you turned your life over to God you became His responsibility for as long as you remain submissive. When you view yourself as a child of God infused with the greatest power in the universe, there is no reason to feel inadequate or inferior. "For you did not receive a spirit that makes you a slave again to fear, but you received the Spirit of sonship. And by him we cry, '*Abba,* Father.' The Spirit himself testifies with our spirit that we are God's children. Now if we are children, then we are heirs—heirs of God and co-heirs with Christ, if indeed we share in his sufferings in order that we may also share in his glory." (Romans 8:15-17)

This could be the most powerful step in the recovery process. It removes the barriers that have prevented God from accomplishing His will in your life. His power will begin to guide and bless as you seek balance and wellness. "If the Lord delights in a man's way, he makes his steps firm; though he stumble, he will not fall, for the Lord upholds him with his hand." (Psalm 37:23-24)

Now that you have dealt with your vertical relationship to God, you are ready to address your horizontal relationships with the other people in your life.

Step 8. List all the people you have hurt and commit to attempt reconciliation with each of them.

When you are too busy, you will inevitably neglect some of the people closest to you, who deserve or have legitimate needs for your time and attention. As you review the history you compiled in step four, many of these people will come to mind.

Members of your immediate family, such as your spouse, children, brother or sister, and aging parents almost certainly would be included. Outside of your family, the list could include old friends you have lost contact with, associates at work, or fellow church members who needed your encouragement and support when they were in crisis. You may not be consciously aware of it, but in the back of your mind, you are carrying a burden of shame for the ingratitude and indifference you have shown people who are (or should be) significant in your life.

An example of remembering one's neglected obligations is in the Old Testament. The Israelis were captives in Persia. One night, King Xerxes could not sleep, apparently because his conscience was bothering him. He ordered his servant to read the record of his administration. One section noted that an Israeli named Mordecai had warned the king of a conspiracy to assassinate him. "'What honor and recognition has Mordecai received for this?' the king asked. 'Nothing has been done for him,' his attendants answered." (Esther 6:3) The king had been so busy attending to the affairs of his high office that he had forgotten the debt of gratitude he owed Mordecai. He relieved his guilty conscience by arranging for Mordecai to be honored.

Who have you offended by your neglect? It has been said that the opposite of love is not hate; it is apathy. When you resent or disparage someone in your mind, your anger against him or her may burn for a while; but then your attitude moves to a deeper level of estrangement. Your heart becomes cold and indifferent toward them. Before attempting reconciliation, it is important that you come to terms with the reasons for your indifference and neglect. Deal with your own resentments first, and then you will be ready to seek reconciliation with the significant others in your life.

Step 9. Seek out the people you have offended and do something specific for them to show your good will, unless the attempt would cause further harm.

Jesus taught the importance of reconciliation and restitution. In His "Sermon on the Mount" He advised anyone who wished to approach God in worship with an offering to go first and make amends with the people he had offended. "Therefore, if you are offering your gift at the altar and there remember that your brother has something against you, leave your gift there in front of the altar. First go and be reconciled to your brother, then come and offer your gift." (Matthew 5:23-24)

In Step 8 you listed everyone you could remember whom you have offended and determined in your heart that you are willing to seek reconciliation. The point was to put yourself in the right frame of mind. Step 9 is the specific and practical outworking of that decision for the sake of other people.

It may not be practical or even desirable to approach everyone on your list. For example, the relationship with a former romantic love partner should be left alone if either of you is married. If the hurt is recent and your approach would only trigger the other person's rage, then it might be wise to give him time to "cool off."

Making amends requires one or both of two actions. In every case, begin with a sincere apology. Do not begin with watered-down statements like, "I'm sorry if I have offended you," or "I'm sorry I hurt you, but I didn't mean to do it." That makes your apology conditional or gives an excuse for your behavior. State specifically what you did wrong and take full responsibility for it, such as, "I was not there for you when you needed me. I failed you, and I am sorry I hurt you."

In many cases, an apology may be all that is needed. In other cases, restitution may be appropriate. If you have been putting other priorities ahead of the relationship to your spouse or children, then you need to make a commitment and plan to spend more time with them. Suggest a specific activity that you know they enjoy and set a date for it to show your good faith. Then move heaven and earth if necessary to keep that date.

Unfortunately, every story does not have a happy ending. Some attempts at reconciliation will not be received positively by the other person involved. Forgiveness is a decision the other person must make, and you can neither control it nor be responsible for it. You can have the satisfaction of knowing that you did your part by apologizing and offering to make restitution.

When you go through this procedure for each person on your list, if appropriate, you will experience healing of old hurts, strengthening of relationships, and release from the burden of shame, guilt and remorse.

Step 10. Continually take a personal inventory and promptly admit wrongdoings.

God wants to give peace to your heart and bless you as you live in obedience to His will. However, He cannot do that if you turn away from Him. "I will listen to what God the Lord will say; he promises peace to his people, his saints—but let them not return to folly." (Psalm 85:8) It is necessary to take stock of your behavior to make sure you are not returning to your old self-centered addictive patterns.

The last three steps repeat some of the actions of the other steps. Their purpose is to emphasize the importance of maintaining the recovery process daily. There are five things to consider when reviewing your personal inventory.

First, consider your needs. Recognize what your basic needs are, such as security, acceptance and love. Determine whether they are being met at least to some extent or if you are experiencing a deficit.

Second, consider your feelings. Are you allowing grief feelings to surface for needs that were not met in the past? It is healthier to bring out grief and work through it than to deny it and leave it buried. Are you experiencing fear? For the workaholic, the fear is usually of failure or missing out on the good life. By keeping in touch with your fears, you can keep them in perspective and deal with them. Most important, how do you feel about people who have caused you pain? Have you forgiven them, or are you allowing resentment to build up in your heart?

Third, consider whether or not you are resorting to your old addictions to attempt to satisfy your needs. Are you lapsing into compulsive, perfectionist behavior, or are you trusting God to meet your needs?

Fourth, consider what you have done that was wrong. What did you do about it? Did you try to cover it up or ignore it? Did you promptly admit the wrongs you have done? If you don't, you will allow shame and guilt to creep back into your life.

Fifth, consider how you are relating to God. Are you making time for prayer and meditation in the Word? Addictive behavior usually stems from willful self-assertion. Are you continuing to submit to God's will? That leads you to the next step.

Step 11. Seek to know God better through prayer and meditation, and ask Him to lead you into His will.

Prayer is essential to the Christian life and the recovery process. "Be joyful always; pray continually; give thanks in all circumstances, for this is God's will for you in Christ Jesus." (I Thessalonians 4:15) There is nothing mysterious or complicated about prayer. It is simply talking to God as you would to any other person, except that you should show respect to His authority as the sovereign ruler of the universe.

See the explanation in Chapter seven of the model prayer Jesus taught His disciples. It is not necessary to repeat this prayer every time you pray. Rather, you can use it as a guide to the basic elements that ought to be in most of your prayers.

In addition to prayer, meditation on the Word of God is essential to finding God's will for your life. God has revealed His will in His Word. It is futile to expect Him to reveal something to you personally that has been clearly revealed in Holy Scripture. You have the responsibility to study the Bible and learn about God's will. David wrote, "I desire to do your will, O my God; your law is within my heart." (Psalm 40:8) Another psalmist wrote, "How can a young man keep his way pure? By living according to your word. I seek you with all my heart; do not let me stray from your commands. I have hidden your word in my heart that I might not sin against you." (Psalm 119:9-11)

Christian meditation is different from the approach taught by Eastern mysticism. Eastern mysticism tells you to empty your mind and open yourself up to spirit guides, or to your inner self. Christian meditation, on the other hand, fills your mind with the Word of God. As you read a scripture passage, turn it over in your mind repeatedly until you have committed it to memory. Then reflect on each word. Think about what it means, how it relates to other scripture passages, and how it applies to your life.

Prayer and meditation are means to a greater end. Their purpose is to enable you to know God and to develop a personal relationship with Him. "I will give them a heart to know me, that I am the LORD." (Jeremiah 24:7)

Step 12. By consistently practicing these principles, become an example that others who are suffering from busy-ness addiction can follow; and lead them to the new life in Christ that you have discovered.

An addiction is a powerful force that is almost impossible to overcome without outside help. In the final analysis, a spiritual transformation is necessary to provide any hope for recovery. That is what the preceding steps are designed to accomplish. The only source of power strong enough and reliable enough to give lasting deliverance is God.

However, God delights to work through people who are willing to serve Him. The best-qualified person to help someone caught in an addictive syndrome is one who is recovering from the same or a similar addiction. "Praise be to the God and Father of our Lord Jesus Christ, the Father of compassion and the God of all comfort, who comforts us in all our troubles, so that we can comfort those in any trouble with the comfort we ourselves have received from God." (II Corinthians 1:3-4) By reaching out to others, you are actually confirming and completing your own recovery.

These 12 steps are not just simple "how to" lessons that can be used once and then put aside. They are guidelines for a new way of living, a routine that you must follow for the rest of your life. Compared to what you have been experiencing in your addiction, the quality of your life will dramatically improve. You will not want to live any other way once you have let them restore balance and wellness to your life.

CHAPTER 11

The Way Back to Balance

THE ERROR OF THE FORK

By now you realize that the way you have been going with your excessively busy lifestyle is not taking you to the goal of fulfillment, satisfaction, wellness and balance. You have made what is sometimes called the "error of the fork in the road." At some point in your life you made a wrong turn. Led astray by the culture and your own desires, you lost your perspective on what is most important in life. Although you have made several more turns, you are still headed in the same general direction, going farther away from the kind of life you truly want. What is worse, you are running out of fuel and time. If something does not change, you will end up at a dead-end somewhere that you do not want to be.

The only way to avoid that result is to make a decision. You must stop going in the direction you are headed and go back to the fork in the road where you made the wrong turn in the first place. Then you will be on the road to a life that is worth living.

A CASE STUDY OF THE JOURNEY TO WELLNESS

Jesus told a story about a young man who made a journey like that. It is the parable of the prodigal son, recorded in Luke 15:11-32. Transcending time and culture, his experience typifies the steps a person goes through when he turns his life away from God and then finds his way back again. The first six steps took him away from God and the last seven steps brought him back.

Step 1: Tunnel Vision (verse 12)

The young man became detached from his family and his father in particular. Instead of examining his own heart, he blamed his responsibilities at the family farm and being under his father's authority for his feelings of dissatisfaction. Eventually he became preoccupied with his "problem." His relationship with his father became of little importance to him. Finally, he became fatalistic, assuming that his destiny and hope for fulfillment must be in some far country.

The result was that he became desensitized to the implications of his actions. According to the customs of Jewish culture, a father could either leave his estate to his heirs in a will, or he could begin to pass on part of the estate to the heirs before his death in the form of gifts. Knowing this, the younger son brazenly asked his father to give him his portion of the estate before his death. He was desensitized to the pain he caused other members of his family.

Step 2: Abandonment of a Biblical World View (verse 13a)

His motive became clear in just a few days. He wanted to leave his father and travel to a far country. In effect, he wanted to break the fellowship he had with his father and be free to form associations that he knew would not meet his father's approval. He wanted to be in control of his life away from his father's influence and authority. The inevitable result was that he adopted a worldview opposite to the one his father had taught him.

Step 3: Psychological and/or Personality Disorder (verse 13)

Ironically, when the young man took control of his life away from his father, he lost control of himself. Instead of using the money wisely to build a good life, he wasted his inheritance on a wild, self-indulgent lifestyle. He compulsively spent his money on pleasurable experiences until he found himself impoverished by his own destructive behavior.

Step 4: Reactive versus Proactive Response to Life (verse 14)

First the young man was unable to manage the events in his life that should have been under his control. Then events occurred over which he had little or no control. A famine occurred in the whole region. With nothing in reserve to fall back on, he could only react to his situation. Typical reactions to crisis are either fight or flight. Both are stressful, especially when one is not in a position to do either and the response must be suppressed.

Step 5: Compromise (verse 15)

In desperation, the young man took the only job he could find, hiring himself out as a farm worker responsible for feeding pigs. Here is another irony. He left home and traveled to the far country to avoid working with his father on the family farm. The work he did for his father was honorable and appropriate for a man of his social standing; but feeding pigs was not. For a Jewish man, this was the most degrading work imaginable, since pigs were considered unclean animals by the Jews and not fit to eat. Anyone coming into regular contact with them would be continually defiled. His work required him to violate his conscience and compromise any scruples he might have left.

Step 6: Psychological/Spiritual Bankruptcy (verse 16)

The prodigal eventually became so hungry that he would have eaten the food he was feeding to the pigs. He had reached the end of himself and his resources. He had sunk as low as he could go. People in this state often experience addictions, obsessive/compulsive behavior, depression, panic attacks, burnout, and chronic physical illnesses.

CONVICTION

At this point, something began to change in the young man's mind. Totally disillusioned by his disastrous attempt to enjoy the "good life" and "have it all" in the far country, he reconsidered the way he had been thinking. His "price tags" had changed. Previously, he valued the freedom from restraint and the pleasures his money could buy more than fellowship with his father and a life of responsible service under his authority. What he had considered of utmost importance he finally regarded as worthless and empty. Fellowship with his father, which had seemed unimportant before, became valuable to him again. He had misjudged his priorities. His life was hardly worth living any more. He needed a way out of his situation. At last, he was ready for change in his life. The value he would receive from making the change would be greater than what he would give up to make the change. That is the necessary condition for meaningful, lasting change.

Step 1: Realization of the Problem (verse 17)

He took the first step back to his father when he "came to his senses." During the first six steps, he had been in denial. He thought he was in control of his life. He assumed he could manage any problems created by his narcissist lifestyle. He could have changed the direction of his life, but he saw no pressing need to do it. He did not realize how much trouble he was creating for himself.

When he arrived at a dead-end in the pigsty, he had to admit to himself that his life had been going in the wrong direction. He remembered how even the hired men on his father's estate always had plenty of food to eat. If he remained where he was, he would starve to death. He realized that he had made a bad decision when he left his father's house.

Step 2: Admission of the Problem (verse 18)

The prodigal made a firm resolve to return to his father and admit that he had sinned. He made progress toward changing his life because he moved from the idea that he "should" change to the definite commitment, "*I will* set out and go back to my father." He did not leave himself an excuse for failure by merely saying, "I will try…"

Neither did he exempt himself from blame by projecting it onto someone else. He could have blamed his brother's bad attitude for his leaving. His brother did have a negative attitude toward him, but it was no excuse for hurting his father. He could have complained that the people in the far country took advantage of him when he had money and then refused to help him when he got into trouble. That would have been true; but it was his decision that put him in the far country in the first place.

The young man took the blame himself and admitted, "I have sinned against heaven and against you." He acknowledged the absolute moral standards that he had violated in his unrestrained lifestyle. He also became sensitized to the hurt he had inflicted on his father who loved him.

Step 3: Repentance of the Problem (verse 19)

Repentance is a change of mind. This young man who had arrogantly demanded from his father what was due him in his inheritance came to regard himself as "…no longer worthy to be called your son," and decided to ask his father to "…make me like one of your hired men." Not only did the prodigal reveal a dramatic change in the way he was thinking, but he also displayed an attitude of true humility, both of which are necessary for lasting change to occur. He did not demand the right to be in control of his life any more, but was willing to relate to his father in a servant role under his authority. The apostle, Paul, expressed this idea in I Corinthians 6:20, "You were bought at a price. Therefore honor God with your body."

Step 4: Return to a Biblical Worldview (verse 20a)

Being under his father's care and provision was no longer something to escape from in the young man's mind. Rather, it became the thing he wanted most in life. He was willing to surrender his freedom to reclaim it. He considered being a servant to his father the most rewarding and satisfying role he could play in life. The moral values and standards that were repugnant and repressive to him before had been proven to be true and right. "So he got up and went to his father." He was willing to embrace his father's worldview with all its restraints and expectations. He trusted his father to deal fairly and kindly with him as he always had done with his hired servants.

> *Jesus said, "Come to me, all you who are weary and burdened, and I will give you rest. Take my yoke upon you and learn from me, for I am gentle and humble in heart, and you will find rest for your souls. For my yoke is easy and my burden is light."*
> *(Matthew 11:28-30)*

Step 5: Reconciliation (verses 20b-21)

The prodigal son did not anticipate the response he would get from his father. He expected recriminations, and had mentally prepared himself to be relegated to the status of a hired hand.

Actually, the father had remained steadfast in his love for his son. As soon as the son approached his home his father saw him, which clearly implies that the father had been watching for him and eagerly anticipating his return. Wisely, he had not sent messengers to the far country to check on the son and give him aid. If he had done so, it would have established a co-dependent relationship, and the son would have been enabled to remain in the far country indefinitely.

Filled with compassion, the father ran to his son, threw his arms around him and kissed him, as was the custom in the Near East. The prodigal son and his father were reconciled. Once he had reconciled with his father, the prodigal had a good basis for restructuring all of his personal relationships in a healthy manner.

Step 6: Forgiveness (verse 22)

True repentance always leads to forgiveness. The father already had a disposition to forgive his son. As soon as he heard his son's confession and saw his change of heart, he freely forgave him. He did not recriminate or defer forgiveness until the son had proved himself on probation. His forgiveness was immediate and complete. By giving his son the best robe, the ring on his finger and the sandals on his feet, the father demonstrated that he was restoring him to full sonship and a place of honor and respect in the family.

When one has been forgiven by God, he has an obligation to forgive others. Jesus admonished his disciples, "For if you forgive men when they sin against you, your heavenly Father will also forgive you. But if you do not forgive men their sins, your Father will not forgive your sins." (Matthew 6:14-15) The natural response to receiving forgiveness from God is willingness to forgive others, resulting in the healing of personal relationships.

Step 7: Restoration of Joy (verses 23-24)

The prodigal son lost his joy when he became rebellious against his father and began to dream of the far country. He may have enjoyed the pleasures of sin for a while, but the experience left him bankrupt and more miserable than ever. When he returned to his father's house and experienced his father's love and forgiveness, he experienced joy again, lasting joy.

His father was full of joy over his son's return and ordered a celebration. In the parable of the lost sheep Jesus said, "...there will be more rejoicing in heaven over one sinner who repents than over ninety-nine righteous persons who do not need to repent." (Luke 15:7) The father's joy is contagious. Living in the father's house brings one into the presence of joy.

The absence of joy is a clear indication that one has lost contact with God and that his life is out of balance. The apostle, Paul, expected joy to characterize the Christian life. "Rejoice in the Lord always. I will say it again: Rejoice!" (Philippians 4:4)

It is difficult to understand how one can remain joyful when life's circumstances are harsh. Indeed, if one focuses on his immediate circumstances it will be impossible to remain joyful. Joy can be sustained only when one turns his mind beyond his immediate circumstances to the future that God has planned for every believer. No matter what happens, deep down in one's soul there can be sustaining confidence that God is in control; and in the end He will make everything work out for the believer's own good and for His glory. That conviction is the basis for continuing joy under any circumstances.

IF NOT YOU, WHO? IF NOT NOW, WHEN?

Perhaps you saw some parallels between your experience and the story of the prodigal son. Traditionally, the prodigal has been identified with non-believers, and certainly that is appropriate. However, the fact that he was in the father's house and then left it makes his story a nearly perfect parallel of a backslidden believer. The main point of the story is the steadfast love of the father for sinners, whoever they may be, and his willingness to forgive them when they repent and return to him.

Even if you are a Christian, a Christian leader or a pastor, you could have wandered away from close fellowship with your heavenly Father. The subtle influences of Western culture and your own drives and ambitions may have drawn you to the far country. You find yourself caught up in the atmosphere of driven-ness. You crowd your schedule with more activities than you can possibly manage and still keep your peace and joy. You may be busy serving God and your fellow man, but you don't have much time left to meet the needs of your family or to maintain a consistent devotional life in communion with the God you are trying to serve.

If you continue on the path you are traveling, you will eventually reach a crisis point in your family, your health, your emotional and spiritual life. Either your husband or wife will sue you for divorce or both of you will settle for a dead marriage of convenience, with little love or passion left in it. Your children will grow up feeling that they are not important to you. That can lead to resentment, rebellion, complexes, personality disorders, poor self-image and possibly a breakdown of the parent-child relationship. Excessive busy-ness can take its toll on your physical health, leading to chronic fatigue, burnout, heart attack, and a host of stress-related diseases. Emotionally you could become tense and irritable, anxious or depressed. Worst of all, when you are too busy to spend time alone with God, you will become spiritually bankrupt and alienated from God.

Like the prodigal, you can leave the path leading away from the Father whenever you decide to do it. You can wait until the crises force you out of denial when you hit bottom, or you can come to your senses now while there is still something left in your life and relationships that you have not damaged or destroyed by your excessive busy-ness. The Father is waiting for you with compassion and forgiveness in His heart, but even He cannot make the decision to change for you. You are the only one who can do that.

When you decide that balance and wellness in daily fellowship with God are more valuable to you than whatever rewards you are getting from your busy-ness addiction, then you are ready for meaningful and lasting change. It is difficult to change habits of scheduling, relating to other people, eating and exercising. God will give you the grace and power to change when you come to Him in humility and submit yourself to His authority. Your way back to Him is the same path the prodigal son followed. Make the decision, "*I will* set out and go back to my father."

End Notes/Sources

Chapter 1

Brown, Colin. *Philosophy and the Christian Faith* (London: The Tyndale Press, 1969).

Bullfinch's Mythology (New York: Gramercy Books, 1979).

Cannon, William Ragsdale. *History of Christianity in the Middle Ages: From the Fall of Rome to the Fall of Constantinople* (Nashville: Abingdon Press, 1960).

Cumont, Franz. *Oriental Religions in Roman Paganism* (New York: Dover Publications, 1956 [1911]).

Grice L. Shelley. *Church History in Plain Language: Updated 2nd Edition* (Nashville: Thomas Nelson, 1982).

Jones, W.T. *A History of Western Philosophy* (New York: Harcourt, Brace & World, Inc., 1952).

Lasch, Christopher. *The Culture of Narcissism* (New York: W. W. Norton and Company, 1979).

Latourette, Kenneth Scott. *A History of Christianity* (New York: Harper & Row, 1953).

Lucas, Henry S. *The Renaissance and the Reformation: Second Edition* (New York: Harper & Row, 1960).

Noll, Mark A. *Turning Points: Decisive Moments in the History of Christianity* (Grand Rapids, Michigan: Baker Academic, 1997, 2000).

Nash, Ronald H. *Christianity & the Hellenistic World* (Grand Rapids, Michigan: Zondervan Publishing House, 1984).

Phillips, Timothy R. and Dennis L. Okholm, Editors. *Christian Apologetics in the Postmodern World* (Downers Grove, Illinois: InterVarsity Press, 1995).

Rose, H. J. *Religion in Greece and Rome*, (New York: Harper & Row, 1959).

Schaeffer, Francis A. *How Should We Then Live? The Rise and Decline of Western Thought and Culture* (Old Tappan, New Jersey: Fleming H. Revell Co., 1976).

Sire, James W. *The Universe Next Door* (Downers Grove, Illinois: InterVarsity Press, 1976).

Ulansey, David. *The Origins of the Mithraic Mysteries: Cosmology & Salvation in the Ancient World* (New York: Oxford University Press, 1989).

Chapter 2

[1] "Less Fun, Less Sleep, More Work: An American Portrait," National Sleep Foundation, March 27, 2001, www.sleep foundation.org/PressArchives/lessfun_lesssleep.html.
[2] "Drowsy America," *Time Magazine*, Dec. 17, 1990.
[3] Archibald D. Hart, *The Hidden Link between Adrenaline and Stress* (Dallas: Word Publishing, 1995), pp. 21-22.
[4] Shad Helmstetter, *Choices* (New York: Pocket, 1989), p. 35.

Chapter 3

[1] David Brooks, "The Organization Kid," *Atlantic Monthly* (*The Atlantic Online*, printed version), April 2001, p. 7.

[2] *Ibid.*

[3] *Ibid.*, p. 52.

[4] *Ibid.*

[5] *Ibid.*, p. 53.

[6] John T. Bruer, *The Myth of the First Three Years* (New York: The Free Press, 1999, p. 75.

[7] Hillary Rodham Clinton, *It Takes A Village: And Other Lessons Children Teach Us* (New York: Touchstone, 1996), pp. 57-59.

[8] Bruer, *op. cit.*

[9] *Ibid.*, p. 85.

[10] *Ibid.*, p. 86.

[11] *Ibid.*, p.92.

[12] *Ibid.*, p. 95.

[13] *Ibid.*, p. 105.

[14] Alison Gopnik, Andrew Meltzoff, and Patricia Kuhl, *The Scientist in the Crib: What Early Learning Tells Us about the Mind* (New York: Perennial, 1999), p.183.

[15] Bruer, *op. cit.* p. 119.

[16] Jeffrey Kluger with Alice Park, "The Quest for a Super Kid," *Time*, April 30, 2001, p. 52.

[17] Bruer, *op. cit.* p. 63.

[18] Kluger and Park, *op. cit.* p. 54-55.

[19] Bruer, *op. cit.*, p. 147.

[20] *Ibid.*, pp. 144-152.

[21] Kluger and Park, *op. cit.* p. 53.

[22] Kluger and Park, *op. cit.* p. 52.

[23] Walter Kirn with Wendy Cole, "Whatever Happened To Play?" *Time*, April 30, 2001, p. 57.

[24] *Ibid.*, p. 58.

[25] *Ibid.*, p. 57.

[26] Alvin Rosenfeld and Nicole Wise, *The Overscheduled Child: Avoiding the Hyper-Parenting Trap* (New York: St. Martin's Griffin, ©2000), p. 132.

[27] Peter Carey, "Fixing Kids' Sports," *U.S. News and World Report*, June 7, 2004, pp. 44-53. For more information contact the National Alliance For Youth Sports, 2050 Vista Parkway, West Palm Beach, FL 33411, e-mail: nays@nays.org, web site: http://www.nays.org. Other recommended resources: *Why Johnny Hates Sports* by Fred Engh, Square One Publishers, 2002, ISBN 075700041X; *Just Let the Kids Play* by Bob Bigelow, Tom Moroney and Linda Hall, Health Communications, 2001, ISBN 1558749276.

[28] Brooks, *op. cit.* p. 1.

[29] *Ibid.*, pp. 3, 16.

[30] *Ibid.*, p. 13.

[31] Rosenfeld and Wise, *op. cit.*, p. 135.

Chapter 4

Bioce, James Montgomery. *Philippians: An Expositional Commentary* (Grand Rapids, Michigan: Zondervan Publishing House, 1971).

Guiness, Os. *The Call: Finding and Fulfilling the Central Purpose of Your Life* (Nashville: Word Publishing, 1998).

Weaver, Richard M. *Ideas Have Consequences* (Chicago: University of Chicago Press, 1948).

Chapter 5

[1] R. James Steffen, "How to Stop Wasting Time—Experts' Advice," *U.S. News & World Report*, 1982, p. 51.

[2] *Ibid.*, p. 52.

[3] William Onken, Jr. and Donald L. Wass, "Management Time: Who's Got the Monkey?" *Harvard Business Review*.

Chapter 7

1 Alfred Edersheim, *The Life and times of Jesus the Messiah* (MacDonald Publishing Company), pp. 388-389.

2 Norval Geldenhuys, *Commentary on the Gospel of Luke* (Grand Rapids, Michigan: Wm. B. Eerdmans Publishing Company, 1972), pp. 315-317.

3 Dallas Willard, *The Spirit of the Disciplines: Understanding How God Changes Lives* (Harper San Francisco: New York, 1988), p. 166.

4 Betsy Streisand, "Tuning Out TV," *U.S. News & World* Report: Volume 136, Number 18, May 24, 2004, page 48.

Chapter 8

1 Merrill F. Unger, "The Temple of Solomon," *Unger's Bible Dictionary* (Chicago: Moody Press, 1966), pp. 1076-77.

2 Udo Erasmus, *Fats that Heal Fats that Kill* (Burnaby, BC: Alive Books, 1993), p. 100.

3 *Ibid.*, p. 111.

4 For more information see Jane E. Allen, "Snack Makers Targeting Trans Fats," *The Los Angeles Times,* September 30, 2002.

5 For more information see "The Nation: FDA Studies Cancer Risk from Baked, Fried Foods," *The Los Angeles Times,* October 1, 2002.

6 Erasmus, *op. cit.,* p. 128.

7 *Ibid.*, p. 47.

8 Nicholas Perricone, M.D., *The Perricone Prescription* (New York: Harper Resource, 2002), p. 61.

9 *Ibid.*, p. 47.

10 *Ibid.*, p. 35.

11 Barry Sears with Bill Lawren, *Enter The Zone* (New York: Harper Collins Publishers, Inc., 1995), pp. 28-30.

12 Erasmus, *op. cit.,* p. 212.

[13] *Ibid.*, p. 210.

[14] Geoffrey Cowley, "A Better Way To Eat," *Newsweek*, January 20, 2003.

[15] For a lively discussion of this subject, see *Food Politics: How the Food Industry Influences Nutrition and Health* by Marion Nestle, University of California Press, March 2002, ISBN 0520224655.

[16] Katy Kelly, "The Brie and Merlot Diet," *U.S. News and World Report*, March 7, 2005, p. 54.

[17] *Ibid.*

[18] *Ibid.*

[19] Perricone, *op. cit.*, pp. 70-71.

Chapter 9

[1] Emily Johnson, "No Bending or Twisting," *U.S. News & World Report*, June 21, 2004, p. 74.

Appendix

The following resources are recommended for further reading and study on diet and nutrition:

Books

Agatston, Arthur, M.D., *The South Beach Diet: The Delicious, Doctor-Designed, Foolproof Plan for Fast and Healthy Weight Loss* (Emmaus, Pennsylvania: Rodale Press, 2003), hardback ISBN 1579546463, 310 pages.

Heavin, Gary and Carol Colman, *Curves: The Power to Amaze Yourself* (New York: G. P. Putnam's Sons, 2003), hardback ISBN 0399150617, 335 pages.

Perricone, Nicholas, M.D., *The Perricone Prescription: A Physician's 28-Day Program for Total Body and Face Rejuvenation* (New York: Harper Resource, 2002), hardback ISBN 0060188790, 274 pages.

Sears, Barry, Ph.D., with Bill Lawren, *Enter The Zone: A Dietary Road Map To Lose Weight Permanently, Reset Your Genetic Code, Prevent Disease, Achieve Maximum Physical Performance, Enhance Mental Productivity* (New York: Harper Collins, 1995), hardback ISBN 0060391502, 328 pages.

Willett, Walter, Dr. and P. J. Skerrett, *Eat, Drink and Be Healthy: The Harvard Medical School Guide to Healthy Eating* (Free Press, 2002), paperback ISBN 0743223225, 304 pages.

Web Sites

Barry Sears: www.zonediet.com
Curves International: www.curvesinternational.com
Nicholas Perricone: www.nvperriconemd.com
South Beach Diet: www.SouthBeachDiet.com
Walter Willett: www.hsph.harvard.edu/facres/wlltt.html